THE MEDIEVAL KITCHEN

THE MEDIEVAL KITCHEN

A Social History with Recipes

Hannele Klemettilä

REAKTION BOOKS

REAKTION BOOKS
Published by Reaktion Books Ltd
33 Great Sutton Street
London EC1V 0DX, UK

www.reaktionbooks.co.uk

Printed and bound in China
by C&C Offset Printing Co., Ltd

British Library Cataloguing in Publication Data
Klemetillä, Hannele.
The medieval kitchen: a social history with recipes.
1. Cooking, Medieval – Europe, Western.
2. Food habits – Europe, Western – History – To 1500.
I. Title
641.5′94′0902-dc23

ISBN 978 1 86189 908 8

CONTENTS

1 The Marquise of Montferrat offers a variety of chicken dishes to her royal admirer, King Philip II Augustus of France. From a 15th-century edition of Giovanni Boccaccio's *The Decameron*.

PREFACE

Medieval cooking is in fashion these days. All across Great Britain and the rest of Europe, medieval feasts are being organized, while new books and studies on the subject are appearing in rapid succession. Even so, misconceptions about medieval food culture remain surprisingly entrenched. It is generally assumed that unpalatable, unwholesome food, lacking variety or seasoned beyond bearing, was eaten on a daily basis in the Middle Ages. The lower classes supposedly lived on dry crusts of bread and watery vegetable soup in which, with luck, the odd piece of something solid floated; and this only in the best of times, when the populace was not literally wasting away from hunger and deprivation. On feast days people allegedly gorged themselves to the point of bursting. More often than not, the meat they ate was rank or hopelessly salty.

According to present-day, stereotypical perceptions, the idle aristocracy in the Middle Ages glutted themselves to excess inside their castles in greasy-jawed overindulgence in red meat, swilling strong, spiced wine for days on end while becoming addicted to alcohol and incapacitated by gout. At the tables of the upper classes, too, the meat was often rotten – or so the story goes – while attempts were made to conceal its rancid flavour with copious amounts of costly spices.

Besides being substandard, flavourless or excessively flavoured, medieval food was allegedly often also pungent, pulpy or downright repulsive. Cooking methods were rudimentary, if not peculiar. People's table manners at the time were utterly revolting; as a result, the late medieval moralists put together etiquette guides and conduct books, which nevertheless fell by the wayside – around the dinner table, barbarism and loutishness reigned unchallenged.

My aim in this book is to acquaint today's reader with the medieval kitchen, to set any fallacies straight and to talk about the prevailing customs, attitudes and ideologies attached to food. My focus is the late Middle Ages (c. 1300–1550), which at present provide us with a greater number of primary sources and information on food culture than the earlier Middle Ages. Geographically the narrative is set throughout Europe.

The recipes and particulars of the medieval food culture covered in this book stem from primary, late medieval source material as well as up-to-date research. The key primary sources of the history of food in the Middle

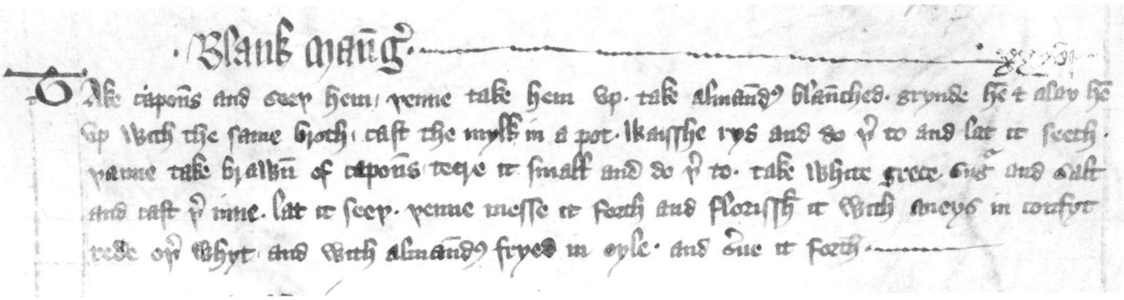

2 Recipe for 'Blank Mang', a dish combining milk, rice, almonds, chopped meat and sugar, in the *Forme of Cury*, one of the oldest known English cookery manuscripts, compiled *c.* 1390 by the master cooks of Richard II. The manuscript contains 196 recipes. The word 'cury' is the Middle English for 'cookery'.

Ages are manuscripts: cookery books and recipe collections, bills of fare, tax records, ledgers, wills and testaments, diaries, chronicles, various guides, encyclopaedias and fiction. Archaeology is an important discipline in the search for information on the eating habits of the lower classes in the Middle Ages, since the recipes of the poor were normally not recorded. Murals, panel paintings, miniatures, woodcuts, tapestries and stained glass also offer useful information. The sources complement each other, and it is important to juxtapose all the available information, as written references can sometimes lead to quite different conclusions than those based on archaeological findings.

Medieval cookery books and recipes are difficult for modern readers because punctuation marks are often missing from the original text: words and phrases are written together in long litanies. Recipes are not always identified by name, and the instructions can be brief, laconic or vague. Nor has every cooking process been put into writing – dough-making and bread-baking, for instance, are rarely described. Quantities, times and temperatures are often left out as well – 'more liberally', 'a little', 'as needed' or 'to taste' are on many occasions the only guidelines. As a rule, the ingredients are cooked until they are well- or nearly well-done. The simple fact that the Middle Ages were the age of oral communication explains this lack of precision.

Today's food historians of the Middle Ages are therefore in most cases obliged to try out and deduce for themselves the required quantities of ingredients, cooking times and temperatures. In the recipe section I have striven to interpret the

3 Preparation for a feast depicted in the *Prodigal Son Window* (*c.* 1214) at the cathedral of Chartres in northern France.

medieval cooking instructions to the best of
my knowledge, while taking into consideration
the demands of today's home kitchens. In cases
where the medieval cook would have resorted to
the swim bladder of a sturgeon, the implementation of a pestle or the repeated straining of a
concoction through a sieve, I have not hesitated
to suggest the use of gelatine leaves or an electric
blender instead to facilitate food preparation. In
several instances, with regard to the ingredients
in a recipe, I have deemed it best to recommend
slightly different quantities and cooking methods
than those my fellow researchers have proposed
when trying out the same source recipe. I encourage my readers to make use of their past cooking
experience and common sense, and to follow
their personal taste preferences, particularly
when measuring out spices. The recipes in *The
Medieval Kitchen* are intended to please and to
delight the senses!

4 This pastoral scene in the book of hours of John, Duke of Berry, dates from 1416 and depicts the gathering of grain outside Poitiers Castle. However, harvests were by no means always this successful. Towards the end of the Middle Ages hardship and unrest prevailed in Europe. A cooling climate resulted in smaller harvests, and the yield from agriculture no longer met the needs of the growing population. Armed conflicts aggravated the economic difficulties, while the aristocracy taxed their subjects more heavily than before. Wealthy land-owners were able to bank on their substantial flour and bread reserves, whereas ordinary peasants had to subsist on wild plants and other food substitutes in order to survive.

one

AN EPICURIAN PARADISE

In medieval society good food was greatly valued, at princely courts and in humble homes alike. Even everyday fare was expected to be as full-flavoured and varied as possible – at their finest, the Middle Ages were a veritable epicurean paradise.

The social structure in Europe at the time was fiercely hierarchical, and the food consumed exposes, even emphasizes, the prevailing class differences. The diet of the lower classes was based on a regimen of vegetables, grains and dairy products, which were noticeably more common in poorer households than among the upper classes. Pulses and grains met the better part of the protein requirements of the poor; meat and eggs supplied the well-to-do with a diet high in animal proteins. In general, every-day eating was determined by seasonal harvests – that is to say, by the availability of certain food products – and adjusted in accordance with the traditions of feast days or the directives of medical science and the Church.

In ordinary times good-tasting and whole-some food was readily available at every social level, and a peasant in the Middle Ages did not eat a great deal worse than his master landlord. But at the end of the Middle Ages wars and poor harvests led to famine, deepening the divide between rich and poor. In times of shortage the rich continued to eat well; the poor, noticeably less well than before. Even so, the late Middle Ages experienced an era of highly refined culinary artistry. Master chefs conjured up sumptuous feasts for the banquets of the aristocracy, while at the tables of the bourgeoisie and the common people there was likewise little cause for complaint.

At the Tables of the Low-born and the Ruling Classes

Documentation from the year 1493 offers detailed information on the workers' diet at the Indersdorf Monastery in Upper Bavaria. Dinner, taken at midday, usually consisted of barley bread, cabbage and some milk. If the workers had been diligent and well disposed, the reeve may have handed out pieces of fruit, beans and millet, depending on availability. For supper, a milky gruel or cabbage and milk may have been offered. Meat was eaten three times weekly: on Sundays, Tuesdays and Thursdays, when a stew of cooked cabbage and pork was served.

Food in Fantasy, Literature and Art

During the troubled years of the late Middle Ages the thought of food among the lower classes was, more than ever before, linked to fantasies of overabundance — along with a sense of fear and looming danger. Lurking at the backs of people's minds were the general insecurities of life, coupled with the dread of deprivation, deathly plagues and epidemics, and the growing efforts of the Church to retain authority. When famine struck many dreamed about Cockaigne, the land of overabundance, where the days were spent forever feasting.

In medieval popular culture the subject of eating, like other bodily functions, was often dwelled upon at length. Partly in disapproval of this trait, some educational mystery plays targeted at the masses included jokes about food and other similar themes that were easily grasped by the public: in scenes of martyrdom brutal pagan executioners likened their victims to meatballs, sausages and other edibles, lacing their dialogue with commonplace expressions and kitchen jargon suffused with macabre gallows humour.

Eating and drinking were of considerable importance in the literary fiction and fine art of the aristocracy, where food and all that it stood for served to define the relationships and bonds between humans. A shared meal, for instance, was an expression of friendship. A person's wealth and social rank (rich versus poor) or moral composition (devout versus depraved) was also demonstrated through the food he ate.

In the performing arts greedy gluttons were on many occasions given droll but revealing first names such as, say, Friant or Gourmand, Picolardon or Fat Eater, or Menjumatin, the one who eats incessantly, from dawn till dusk. Those who drank excessive amounts of wine were also named accordingly, like Tirevin, Wine Swigger.

Works were dedicated entirely to the quandaries of overindulging in or abstaining from food. One example is Nicholas de la Chesnaye's morality play *The Condemnation of Banquets* (*Condemnation des banquets, c.* 1507), in which the merciless hangman Diet hangs the principal character Banquet on the orders of the female judge Madame Expérience. This stage play passes judgement on overindulging in food and drink, albeit in a rather ambiguous and sarcastic manner.◁

5 Farmhouse kitchen depicted in a medieval manuscript. In the Nordic countries, too, everyday fare in farmhouses was simple, usually consisting of barley and rye bread, gruel or porridge, dried fish and salted meat. Turnips, cabbages, broad beans and onions were cooked together in stews. On special occasions northern peasants feasted on game, bean dishes with meat, and porridge cooked with milk.

The fifteenth-century French popular encyclopaedia *Kalender of Shepherdes* (*Le grant kalendrier et compost des Bergiers*) lists foods commonly eaten by peasants, mentioning, among other things, fish stew, chicken or rabbit stew, bean stew, pork and bean stew, stewed leeks, Brussels sprouts, mutton stew, leg of lamb, veal pie, stewed entrails and cheese tarts. According to the anonymous author of the *Kalender of Shepherdes*, the diet of peasants differed from that of the upper classes mainly in that it included fewer fried or roasted meats and bakery products.

In other words, under normal circumstances, the difference between the diet of lesser noblemen and that of their labourers was not particularly significant. At the tables of the aristocracy, the number of courses was generally greater: for instance, at the head table of the Bavarian

Count Joachim of Oettingen (*d.* 1520), eight courses were brought out at dinner, and six at supper. The servants were given a more limited selection of courses – only three or four – since rice dishes and some of the meat courses were excluded from their fare.

As a rule, meals were taken only twice daily in medieval times, as advocated by moralists and physicians who warned against eating more frequently, since it was considered unhealthy and courted sin. It was also important to be different from animals, which ate throughout the day.

In the early Middle Ages 'dinner' was taken at midday and 'supper' at dusk. Dinner was the main meal, while supper remained a lighter repast with fewer and less complicated courses. As time went by, dinner service at the tables of the upper classes evolved to become more elaborate, and the hour of dinnertime was moved to past midday. Supper, in turn, could be served as late as around seven or eight o'clock in the evening, but it remained a less complex production than dinner. Breakfast was considered excessive and, according to certain learned opinion, inappropriate, especially for a hale and hearty man. Very few particulars on breakfast in the Middle Ages remain with us today, although it was likely to have consisted of a piece of bread and some wine diluted with water. Before retiring for the day, a little spiced wine may have been ingested, something that was customary at the fifteenth-century Savoyard court, for instance.

Indulging on Feast Days

In the Middle Ages, like today, eating well and plentifully was an integral part of celebrating a special occasion. The wealthy were more likely to observe any given event, although others, too, gathered around the festive table whenever the opportunity presented itself – on family occasions such as births, baptisms, betrothals, weddings and burials, and on holy days and during religious festivals. In addition the lower classes celebrated their own work-, slaughter- and harvest-related festivals. Landowners and wealthy members of the bourgeoisie were also known to hand out meals to the poor on important saints' days.

The wealthier the host of a social gathering was, and the higher he ranked, the more elegant, abundant and diverse was the fare at his table. Any excessiveness related to the consumption of food risked drawing sharp criticism; yet the overindulging that took place on special cele-bratory occasions was in general looked upon with tolerance. Extravagance was simply assumed to be in keeping with the nobility's position in society. Miserliness was deemed unseemly or dishonourable. To entertain lavishly was, on the one hand, a required exercise in Christian hospitality: a token of friendship and brotherly love. On the other, it was a means of further asserting a person's worldly authority – a manifestation of wealth, clout and the obli-gations that power and duty imposed upon the host with regard to his guests. The distribution of food among the poor and the needy was one of the seven Christian virtues; therefore the destitute received alms in the form of leftover scraps from the tables of the gentry. Similarly

AT A BANQUET OF THE CITY COUNCIL OF TALLINN

What was served at, say, a Tallinn city council banquet in 1405? Browsing the records of the occasion, one finds included exotic spices such as ginger, pepper, saffron, grains of paradise, cinnamon and cardamom, together with white sugar, salt, raisins and rice. Meats such as roast pork, salted beef, pigs' trotters, mutton, poultry, ham, tongue, salami-type Mettwurst sausages, white pudding and goose are mentioned, while fresh pike, Baltic herring, perch and assorted preserved fish are listed on the fish order. The records also show various types of bread as well as butter, onions, vinegar, mustard, parsley, garlic, apples, honey and eggs.

For a formal dinner in 1515 mace and other spices for baking were procured. The meat courses comprised roast beef, lamb, chicken, capon, ham, tongue and mettwurst sausages. The fish courses included fresh Dorpat (Tartu) pike and bream as well as assorted preserved fish. The guests were further treated to a variety of breads, cakes, cheeses, butter, bacon, apples, pears, hazelnuts and walnuts.

In 1482 beer is recorded as having been served at the Tallinn guildhalls. Account books from the early sixteenth century mention various types of mild and strong beer, mead and cider, and occasionally also wine from the Rhine Valley.

formal dinners costing more than half a ducat per person. In the region around Florence at the turn of the fourteenth century, meals with more than three courses were prohibited. Attempts were also made to limit the number of attending diners. The application of these laws also strived to point out which foods were appropriate for different social groups. The economic situation of both the individual citizens and the state was of concern as well. In practice, however, the sumptuary laws were of little consequence, and they were repeatedly bypassed and broken.

The Course of Formal Entertaining in High Society

The information available to us today on the social life of the high-ranking members of society in the Middle Ages tickles our imagination with visions of splendour and great detail. When members of the aristocracy or royalty played host at a banquet, the attending guests were seated at their tables according to rank. White table linen covered angular, U-shaped tables. The diners sat along the outer edges of the tables, allowing service and the presentation of dishes to be conducted smoothly from the centre. This also made the entertainment programme easy to follow. The middle table was sometimes called the high table, and the chances are that it was situated atop a raised platform. It was reserved for the host of the event and his guests of honour. Behind this table, a festive covering of cloth hung suspended, emphasizing the standing of the guests of honour while protecting them

the servants of the household were provided for with food left over from feasts.

In the late Middle Ages legislation on general excess was passed in Europe in an effort to curb, among other things, exaggerated spending on food. These sumptuary laws were particularly prevalent in the northern and central city states of Italy. In 1460 the Venetian Senate forbade from draughts. Liquid refreshments were placed on a side table near the middle table, and from here the person in charge of the beverage service carried out his duties. He may have been responsible for a mechanized wine dispenser, and for changing the wine it contained. If the host was of very high standing, a taster would be waiting close at hand. Everything intended for ingestion by royalty was tested for poison. The carver (usually a gentleman of the upper classes) oversaw the carving of the meat at high table. At the surrounding tables, the guests themselves carved their own meat. The art of carving was part of the schooling of a nobleman.

After grace was said, servants wearing the colours of their master would file in, carrying the dishes for the first course. The name of every dish was called out loud. At every place setting there would be a large, round piece of bread to serve as a trencher from which to eat; it would perhaps cover a plate made of wood or metal, silver or gold. Each diner was given his or her own spoon for liquid foods and sauces, and a knife for solid foods. For those of higher standing, larger portions and better-quality food were set aside, compared to the selection those of lesser consequence received. In the event that everyone at table was served the same food, the portions could be sized according to rank. Only the most prominent guests were permitted to have their food served directly onto their personal plates. Elsewhere guests would help themselves from the same platter. Since the diners shared bowls, goblets and salvers, mutual consideration and courtesy was of the essence.

At the banquet tables of the upper classes, several courses followed one after another. The most common number of courses was three; however, at the Savoyard court, for instance, even a formal banquet might have comprised only two courses. In Italy, on the other hand, there could have been as many as eight or twelve. Each course may have included tens of different dishes, brought to the table simultaneously. No guest could possibly help himself to all the dishes, but each individual diner contented himself with whatever was plausibly within his reach. The amount of food and the number of courses served said a great deal about the wealth and standing of the host, as did the quality and distinction of the dishes.

The start of a festive meal was often sweet: sweet pastries, candied fruits, confectionery and sweet wines were served to stir the appetite. The first formal course often consisted of soups and pies; the third, palate-cleansing jellies. At the tables of the gentry, each course, together with its accompaniments, constituted a carefully planned and composed ensemble. The methods of preparing the successive courses did not necessarily have to differ, although it was preferable not to serve a variant of the same basic ingredient twice in a row. A skilled menu planner would be mindful of the symbolism and the order of importance of the meat courses. The high point of a festive meal was usually the roast, around which the entire menu was planned. Meat was pre-eminent among food and dominated the bill of fare at any given time, with the exception of fast days.

The last courses rounded off the meal. These were not part of the repast per se. The dessert, which by its very name indicated that the meal was about to come to an end (it is the

6 A formal meal taken at the court of John, Duke of Berry, brother to King Charles V of France and famed patron of the arts. The Duke had 200 servants and took great pleasure in giving elaborate dinners. According to the chonicler Olivier de la Marche, at the court of Charles the Bold, Duke of Burgundy, mealtimes, even on weekdays, resembled the performance of a great and solemn stage play with its complex table service carried out by numerous staff. The entire court dined in separate halls in groups of ten, meticulously seated according to rank and social standing.

mid-sixteenth-century French past participle of *desservir*: 'to clear the table'), was made up of one or several sweet dishes. This was followed by the *issue de table*, when the guests drank spiced wine and sampled a selection of light pastries, cakes, candied fruits and nuts. Last came the so-called *boute-hors*, which was taken in a different room and usually consisted of spices and confectionery. In other words, the feast was finished in as sweet a fashion as it had begun.

By and large, ordinary people celebrated in essentially the same way, although their feasts comprised fewer courses and dishes, and the sweet starters, desserts and digestives were

ENTREMETS AT ROYAL BANQUETS

The tradition of entremets originated in ancient Rome. At first they were mainly intended to fill the intervals between courses. They also provided long enough breaks from serious eating for the succeeding dishes to be fully appreciated. In the early fifteenth century these diversions became more complex, acquiring an increasingly important role. Their subject-matter could be allegories, moral, religious or pseudo-religious themes, the ages of man, celestial apparitions or mythological beasts.

Common entremets included displays of intricate food compositions and fantasy foods, such as pies from which birds ascended, or towers built from tartlets flying the standards of the invited guests. There could be expertly decorated cakes which the diner, even while cutting into them, took for fish in a pastry crust, and make-believe hedgehogs and porcupines with spines made of silvered almonds. A cooked animal could be presented as living, such as a boar biting an apple. Baked swans were re-dressed in their plumage and decorated with silver and gold. The crowning moment of many a festive meal was a peacock that appeared to be alive: the baked bird, bedecked once more with its feathered costume, was propped upright on a serving platter with the help of rods. A piece of tuft soaked in alcohol may have been placed in its mouth and set alight, creating the illusion that it was breathing fire, when it was brought to table.

The brainchild of Maître Chiquart, who served at the Savoyard court in the fifteenth century, was the feathered epidermis of a peacock wrapped around a baked goose. Similarly the stripped hide of an animal could be filled with minced meat, herbs and spices. A Neapolitan collection of recipes from the late Middle Ages gave advice on how to make two pigeons out of one: the bird's skin was wrapped around a mixture of cheese, eggs, spices and raisins. The opening was sewn together, and the 'new' pigeon was cooked in boiling water. The skinned carcass, in turn, was baked and, halfway through the cooking, coated with a mixture of breadcrumbs and glazed with egg wash. An amalgam of two animals fused into one could also be created. The 'half cock' (*cokagrys* or the *cokentrice*), for example, was well known: it was the upper half of a capon attached to the stuffed hindquarters of a pig.

Illusionary foods were conceived separately for those formal events that coincided with periods of fasting. Among these were sturgeon dressed as veal (*esturgeon contrefait de veau*) from the French household book *Le Ménagier de Paris*; spit-roasted, simulated pieces of meat made from dried fruits and almond paste (*hasteletes of fruyt*), as described in the English cookery book *Forme of Cury*; and imitation cheese tarts from the recipe collection *Le Viandier de Taillevent*. Imitation cheeses were usually made from almond milk and fish broth, and imitation butter from rose water.

The banquets at the Burgundian court in particular were famous for their imaginative entremets. On certain festive occasions an enormous pie would be brought in, harbouring a twelve-member musical orchestra. At the banquet held in honour of Isabella of Portugal in 1430, a live lamb, painted blue with gilded horns, leaped out of an immense pie, followed by Hans the Giant, swathed in the skin of a wild beast. To the delight of the invited guests, the Giant proceeded to grapple with the court jester, Madame d'Or. ◁

7 A royal banquet with entremets, depicted in the *Grandes chroniques de France de Charles V*. Besides denoting sweet and savoury dishes served between two courses of a formal meal, the French word *entremets* also referred to vignettes of entertainment such as music, dance, acrobatic performances and mock fighting.

lacking altogether. The poorest households made do with a single dish of food, which contained, circumstances permitting, meat or fish and vegetables.

Certain festive meals coincided with periods of fasting, at which point variations of favourite meat dishes were created to comply with the observance of the fast. These substitute versions, served at the tables of the upper classes, were often just as tantalizing and impressive as the delicacies brought out under normal circumstances. The food prepared during a period of abstinence was given added sparkle by increasing the quantities of spices and fruit. In upper-class circles the rules and regulations were also known to have been circumvented: the flesh from harbour porpoise and whale could pass for fish, as could beaver tail and certain waterfowl. Throughout a formal dinner coinciding with a period of fasting, the courses of food and the order in which they were served did not deviate from the norm; however, a rather half-hearted stance was taken towards the dishes in general during a fast. That said, fasting and the restrictions it imposed had a positive influence on the development of food preparation and, in particular, the art of cooking fish in the Middle Ages.

It was common for guests at a dinner party to bring their own eating utensils – that is to say, a spoon and a knife – though the spoon did not begin to appear regularly until the fourteenth century. The meat was carved into portions and placed onto a serving platter, after which the diner cut it into bite-sized pieces on his own plate, with his own knife. He held the meat with his fingers and brought the morsels to his mouth in a refined and decorous manner, using three of the fingers on his right hand. Forks were certainly in use, although mainly in the kitchens: they were long-handled and used for transferring chunks of meat from cooking pots to other vessels. The Italians introduced the use of individual dinner forks at the end of the fourteenth century, and it took some 200 to 300 years for the custom to spread to other parts of Europe. For example, the dinner fork arrived in Finland in the sixteenth century under the auspices of Princess Catherine Jagellon of Poland, wife to Duke John of Finland (later King John III of Sweden). Initially the implementation of the fork was linked to certain legendary mishaps.

Since everyone at table ate with their fingers and often from communal platters, particular attention was paid to hygiene during a formal meal. The diners washed their hands before the meal began. This ritual was also a symbolic gesture that made reference to the Last Supper. Hands were also washed and dried during intervals in the meal. At more genteel events, small finger bowls were placed all along the tables; at some fifteenth-century Italian banquets, a selection of no less than three types of finger-rinsing water was offered, giving the diner a choice of lemon, myrtle or mace scent. A long, narrow cloth running down the guests' side of the table might also have been used to cover the principal tablecloth, protecting it from stains and permitting the guests to wipe their fingers and mouths.

European Cookery in the Middle Ages

Europe's medieval kitchen had its origins in ancient Rome. The most significant change

8 In the Middle Ages it was usual to lay a table with a single platter of food, from which each diner would take his portion. In this painting of the Last Supper by Dirk Bouts, a long narrow cloth protects the principal tablecloth and serves as a common napkin.

since antiquity lay in the use of spices, which increased in the Middle Ages. Medieval cookery matured and flourished in the fourteenth and fifteenth centuries, when the compiling of cookery books resumed after a long interval. Dissociation from the gastronomy of antiquity intensified, while the connection to Arabian cuisine remained open through Sicily and Spain. Towns played an important role in the evolution of culinary skills. Paris and the great cities of northern and central Italy, for instance, were significant, since the average standard of living was higher there than elsewhere. In towns the sources of marketplace produce were diverse, and both local and faraway products were readily at hand.

European cookery underwent a state of change in the post-medieval seventeenth century, when spices from the Far East, with the exception of pepper, lost their popularity, while the use of cooking fats increased. Yet many of our present-day recipes, cooking methods and culinary customs originated in the Middle Ages. Medieval foods are not particularly 'odd' or archaic; on the contrary, they have more in common with contemporary cooking than not.

In the late Middle Ages chefs had recourse to more or less the same primary ingredients as today's cooks, with the exception of novelties such as potatoes, tomatoes, sweet peppers, turkey and cocoa, which arrived in Europe in the wake of the Age of Exploration. However, the general

9 The peacock was the showpiece of many an aristocratic feast. It was associated with a number of religious beliefs: its blood was said to expel demons and its flesh was thought to be immune to rotting. And so it became, in the iconography of Christendom, the representation of the Son of God resting in his grave. The peacock was furthermore a symbol of renewal and resurrection, because it shed its feathers in the spring, to promptly grow new ones. On the other hand, this celebrated bird was also associated with certain dark conceptualizations: in fables the peacock was the symbol of vanity, extravagance and self-importance.

sense of taste and evaluation of flavours differed to some degree from modern-day perceptions. The utilization of spices was also more liberal yet finely nuanced in the Middle Ages – East Indian cooking and the flavours and fragrances of Christmastime come to mind. Religion and the edicts of the Church had a significant impact on food, and professional cooks strived to take medical views into consideration as well.

Along with nourishment and flavour, aesthetics were of importance. Particular attention was given to the appearance, colour and garnishing of dishes, especially on festive occasions. A key objective of chefs was to transform the natural look and taste of food products by using a variety of different ingredients, seasonings and colourings in one and the same dish.

Although we may be inclined to think of the cooking methods of medieval times as peculiar, the basic procedures nevertheless remain familiar to us: boiling, frying, roasting and baking. The everyday fare of peasants and the lower bourgeoisie in particular was relatively inexpensive and did not call for complex cooking techniques. The food prepared for the upper classes, on the other hand, required expert skills: through it, it was possible to signal the social position of the lord of the house, and show the guests his respect. Negligence in the kitchen was unacceptable; instead, accuracy and conscientiousness, cleanliness and good order were essential.

The lower classes customarily boiled their food; this meant that the maximum nourishment was derived from even small quantities of produce. The bain-marie cooking technique was also known: grains, pulses, meat and fish in individual containers could be lowered into large pots of water. Pan-frying was more common than oven roasting, since only a small number of households were equipped with ovens. The use of communal ovens was encouraged in order to reduce the risk of fire, and at home pies could be baked successfully over an open flame.

Grilling, roasting and rotisserie cooking were more common cooking methods in urban households and among the aristocracy. The poor consumed less meat anyway, and roasting over an open fire was a most uneconomical way of using cooking heat. Relatively flat items such as fish (before or after being filleted) were suitable for grilling on a plane or in a hinged gridiron, being too thin for the rotisserie skewer.

A combination of cooking methods was commonly used in the kitchens of the upper classes. Several techniques were applied successively to one and the same ingredient – a tendency that is demonstrated in some of the recipes compiled in this book. Browning before simmering, and blanching before grilling, were common procedures. However, a certain amount of food loss in the process made multiple cooking methods too costly for the less wealthy. An Italian recipe grandly illustrates the manifold cooking stages of fowl: the flesh of a partridge is first boiled, then ground in a mortar, then fried in lard and finally simmered in water and almond milk. Yet not all meats were blanched before being grilled or roasted, nor were all roasted foods simmered. Fish and vegetables, too, could be prepared using multiple cooking methods, although with regard to vegetables, parboiling was detrimental from a nutritional point of view, since the cooking liquid was not reserved. It should also be

10 Two kitchen helpers roast meat on a spit in an illustration from the *Luttrell Psalter, c. 1320–40.*

emphasized that people in the Middle Ages favoured particularly well-done food (which was considered healthier and safer than medium-cooked or raw food), although they did eat raw vegetables, salads and fruit as well.

It was not uncommon to cut, crush or purée solid foods, allowing the largest pieces to fit on a spoon. Ultimately the smoothest results were obtained by passing the softened product through a piece of cheesecloth. One reason behind this penchant for reducing food into minute particles is thought to have been the poor condition of people's teeth. However, large parts of the ingredients were chopped, crushed, ground or strained in order to avoid potentially harmful substances. According to expert medical opinion, blending harmful substances with ingredients of a counter-effective nature could neutralize the former. In order for the counter-

effective ingredients to work efficiently, they needed to be in as close contact with the harmful substances as possible – therefore all food had to be broken up into the smallest possible particles. Meat and fish were also often crushed in a mortar.

Pig fat, or lard, derived from the slaughtering process, was used for boiling and frying, as was olive oil. Almond and nut oils as well as flax and poppyseed oils played an important role, particularly in the preparation of food during a fast. Vegetable oil was recommended foremost for frying fish and certain pastries. In order to prolong its shelf life, butter was generously salted and therefore in need of rinsing before use. Butter was used for cooking mainly in northern France, Flanders and England, while olive oil was favoured in Italy, Spain and southern France. In the German states poppyseed oil was valued.

11 Picking olives in the *Tacuinum sanitatis* (1474). The olive tree grows in the temperate climate of the regions around the Mediterranean Sea. Olive trees have been cultivated since prehistoric times. In ancient Greece the olive tree was dedicated to the goddess Athena; in Rome the branch of the olive tree was the symbol of Pax, the goddess of peace. The Bible contains numerous references to the olive tree (as in Genesis 8:11). The oil from the olive was thought to be nourishing, cleansing and calming. In medieval times, apart from being used for cooking, olive oil was used in the treatment of wounds. Lamps were kept burning with olive oil, and it was used as a balm at royal weddings and in the ceremonies of the Christian Church, from baptisms to the Anointing of the Sick.

Just like today, water was used in large quantities during food preparation. Cautious cooks knew better than to trust anything but pure spring water, since wells and rivers might be contaminated. Laundry was washed in rivers, and all sorts of waste ended up in the water. In London the fishermen used the same river water for cleaning fish as the butchers used for rinsing meat, the brewers for making beer and the ordinary citizens for general use. In the countryside things were somewhat better, but care had to be taken all the same. In 1256 the Italian physician Aldobrandino of Siena issued the general recommendation that only clear, non-smelling, flavourless and colourless water be used for cooking – if it failed any of these criteria, the water was polluted in one way or another.

One distinctive feature of medieval cooking that sets it apart from today's techniques was that wheat flour was not used as a binding agent; instead, sauces were thickened by adding the dried, toasted or grilled centre of white bread to the liquid. Besides bread, eggs, ground almonds and occasionally rice flour were used as binders.

Dairy products such as cream or butter were not used to thicken foods. Coagulating agents were derived from animal gristle or the swim bladders of fish.

In the Middle Ages almond milk and acidic liquids enjoyed a more important place in food preparation than they do today. Almond milk was indispensable when cooking during periods of fasting, although it was frequently used in meat dishes as well. Almonds were popular in the Middle Ages anyway, for the peeled, pale almond was beautiful to behold, and the culinary order of the times showed deference to aesthetics and colour symbolism. Among the most commonly used acidic liquids were vinegar, unfermented grape juice or must, wine and acidic fruit juices. Slightly acid flavours were popular, and acidic liquids promoted the preservation of food. Vinegar was also thought to have appetite-boosting properties. Further north, for instance in England, citrus fruit juices were often used in lieu of grape juice, as occasionally were gooseberry or apple juices. Wine, on the other hand, was not used in cooking as commonly as in the South, beer being more important in England. Beer was used in meat dishes or as a

12 Selling offal at a market stall. Due to climatic, economic and cultural factors, the diet of Europeans in the late Middle Ages was at times derived predominantly from animals. The presence of meat in a diet was greatest in the Northern regions, while the diet in the South of Europe was generally somewhat more vegetable-orientated. Game was more highly rated than meat from domestic animals.

broth for poaching fish, and as a basic liquid ingredient in bakery products and fruit dishes. It could also serve as a diluting agent, or simply as seasoning. Having said this, in recipes for the upper classes, wine appeared more commonly than beer.

In the Middle Ages the tastiness and the tartness of a dish were valued first and foremost, and in many instances also the sweetness and the nuances of the seasoning. The salt content of food was not given much attention, nor were the dishes divided into sweet or savoury categories. Since grease enhanced flavours, animal fat such as suet, lard or butter, or alternatively vegetable fat, was added to both sweet and savoury dishes. A sweet flavour was often combined with a contrasting taste. The taste of sweet-and-sour first gained ground in Italy, and soon achieved widespread popularity elsewhere, having already been much appreciated in the ancient cultures of Persia and Rome. The combination of tart and sweet flavours in one and the same dish was also linked to nutritional theories.

The great medieval infatuation with spices is well known. Spices were used in large quantities and varieties, although by no means in order to disguise the taste of rotting food, as is often claimed. The function of spices was to flavour the food attractively; in addition, expensive, exotic spices were an effective indicator of a person's status, providing a further association with the refinement of the Mediterranean world. Spices are elaborated on more thoroughly in chapter Six.

In the Middle Ages, as in the present day, spoilt food was generally not consumed. Especially for the wealthy, only the most select ingredients were good enough, and the rich were able to acquire quality produce throughout the year. Furthermore any attempt to offload bad food or produce was judged extremely harshly. Grocers were kept under strict surveillance, particularly in cities, and to go against the regulations was to be subject to penalization. Various guilds, professional communities and civil servants were in charge of this supervision. In Venice, for instance, fishmongers were obliged to dispose of all spoilt merchandise, and any effort to make old fish appear fresh was a punishable offence. In England oil, beer, wine and flour were inspected to safeguard against misconduct or fraud; ingredients intended for use in aspics and sausages were also subjected to scrutiny. In 1378 the sale of meat was prohibited in London after dusk. Any vendor found guilty of selling rotten meat could expect the stocks, and on the way to his punishment, the wrongdoer would have a decaying piece of meat held under his nose as a warning to others. Already in 1370 the purchase of putrid kitchen leftovers from cooks, intended for pie filling, was prohibited, as was selling ordinary beef pies as venison pies.

Fat Days and Lean Days: Food and Religion

In the Middle Ages religion and the Church defined food choices for everyone. Both rich and poor had to observe the periods of fasting laid down by Catholic authorities. These did not involve the total rejection of anything edible, nor was water fasting or wasting away from hunger expected, but were rather times

Similarities and Disparities amongst European Food Cultures

A country's kitchen reflects its culture, and throughout the course of history, geography has had its impact on the two as regards raw materials, norms, rules and customs. In the Middle Ages the national identities of the European peoples were less defined than today. The urban culture of the times embraced a unified Christian society, where the disparities in eating habits were greater between the social classes than between the nations. Trends and influences trickled downward from the upper classes, as the rising bourgeoisie tried to imitate the style of the aristocracy at their tables.

The medieval kitchen was extremely international, owing to the itinerant nature of food and food culture. Naturally each region had its own specialities, although these were mostly determined by the availability of raw materials, a prerequisite that, in turn, improved towards the end of the Middle Ages. International trade was brisk: spices arrived from the East, exotic fruits from the South, and from the North came scores of fish products. Foods and dishes associated with other countries gained popularity, their foreign names demonstrating the internationalism of the host and his table, alluding to impressions gained on trips abroad and to a desire to stand out or to acquire the refined tastes of high society.

The food culture among the upper classes in particular had many similarities throughout Europe. Several dishes, among them the so-called whitedish (*blancmange, blang mengier* or *bianco mangiare*), were known across the board. The uniformity of the fare among the upper classes is explained by the fact that aristocratic courts travelled from one palace to another, together with their chefs. The wealthy also had better opportunities to overcome any difficulties in procuring food.

The English nobility, for instance, embraced innumerable culinary influences from the geographically close and culturally similar France. Italy, although weak as a state, was a major centre for art and lifestyle, and impressions from that region flowed into England as trade, diplomatic relations and cultural connections intensified. People travelled to Italy for educational as well as religious purposes. Spain and the Arab countries, in turn, influenced the Italian kitchen. Cultural interaction was lively along the northern latitudes as well; the Scandinavian and Finnish cuisines were highly influenced by Central Europe, although many trends and novelties took their time arriving in the Nordic countries. The Hanseatic League traded briskly in food products up and down the Baltic Sea. Educational journeys to the South were undertaken as well, while foreign merchants, noblemen and representatives of the Church progressed northwards, bringing with them novelties and a whiff of the outside world. ◁

of abstinence from meat and other animal products such as suet or lard, butter, cheese, milk and eggs. Fasting was aimed at cleansing the spirit and soul, and practised in remembrance of the death of Christ.

The longest periods of fasting were those preceding the great celebrations of the liturgical year: the forty-day Lenten Season beginning on Ash Wednesday and ending on Easter eve, and the fasts of Advent leading up to Christmas. The number of meatless days varied through the course of the Middle Ages. At one point the Church demanded four fasting seasons, each

lasting forty days. The eves of holy days were also meatless days. Fridays and Saturdays were initially designated weekly fasting days, although as time went by, Fridays became more firmly anchored in the tradition, commemorating the day Christ was nailed to the cross. According to some, fasting should also be conducted on Mondays and Wednesdays, leaving meat to be eaten on Sundays, Tuesdays and Thursdays only. Be that as it may, in late medieval Europe fasting in one form or another was carried out every week of the year. Of all the days in the year, 140 or more were consecrated to fasting, during

13 Two fish symbolize fasting in this painting by Hieronymus Bosch. Christian dogma early on adopted views from other religions on the differentiation between clean and unclean foods. The factions grew more moralizing in nature, as ways were sought in which the individual could further cleanse himself to become more perfect before God. The early Christian Church maintained that abstinence from meat was beneficial to the soul. Isidore of Seville (c. AD 560–636) praised the moral advantage of fasting and wrote that eating meat fuelled sinful quests for carnal pleasures.

which time a true Christian was obliged to eat meagrely – fish and vegetables – in remembrance of the death of Christ.

Within the religious orders fasting was an integral part of asceticism, believed to keep the desires of the flesh in check. Directives on fasting differed between the various monasteries or convents. Within certain orders a regimen predominantly void of meat, fish and vegetables was upheld. Up until the beginning of the thirteenth century the diet of monks and nuns in England remained extremely frugal: contemplatives were not allowed to eat any form of animal meat, and they were only given one main meal per day. The unwell and elderly residents of an abbey were, however, permitted fowl and occasionally also other types of meat, as were the official representatives of the order. By the same token, not all early medieval monasteries upheld this highly abstemious regimen, at least not if the chronicles of Friar Ekkehard IV are to be believed, since they tell about the rich and varied fare at the Abbey of St Gall in Switzerland.

To the ordinary layperson fasting meant the observance of a certain diet during a certain period of time, and only the most devout ascetics engaged in the strictest forms of abstinence. Yet by no means all members of the clergy idealized extreme fasting. Erasmus of Rotterdam (c. 1466–1536) recommended moderation instead, particularly for the young. 'Those who force a youth to fast are, in my opinion, no better than those who force upon him too much food. Fasting holds back the development of a young body, while too much food, again, saps the spiritual fortitude.' Erasmus himself detested fish.

14 Angels serve food to St Dominic and the monks in this painting by Fra Angelico, c. 1430. The pleasures of eating were reduced to a minimum in medieval monasteries.

His aversion to it stemmed from the time he was a student in Paris, living at the Collège de Montague.

The abstinence imposed by fasting was undoubtedly a little less disagreeable to the wealthy, since palace chefs developed delicious substitutes for their masters' tables. In the fifteenth century Maître Chiquart, head chef at the Savoyard court, put together a list of alternative menu suggestions compatible with fasting:

Braised German capon / German fish stew
Braised Savoyard chicken / Savoyard fish stew
Roast beef in river lamprey sauce / Entrails of
large fish
Wheat frumenty and game / Rice with dolphin,
butter-crust pastries and puddings
Almond milk pudding, partridge in wine sauce /
Eel in brown sauce
Wild boar / Bacon-wrapped tench
Rabbit in pepper sauce / Fried fish in pepper sauce
Capon soup / Fish soup
Parmesan meat pies / Parmesan fish pies

Maître Chiquart had good reason for delving into the art of preparing substitute foods, since his master Amadeus VIII (1383–1451), the first Duke of Savoy, took an interest in religion: from 1439 to 1449 the Duke served as the last antipope under the name Felix V.

In theory the edicts on fasting and the potential presence of religious persons had to be taken into consideration at every meal; this was done by including a fish alternative to the meat course on days when meat was otherwise permitted. However, this rule may well have been disregarded even in the Church's own circles, especially on formal occasions. In general, and for a long time, the diet of the clergy and the religious elite in particular remained similar to that of the lay upper classes.

The dictates on fasting were of course beneficial to a person's physical health, although physicians of the time did not as a rule regard fish and vegetables as particularly nutritious. Furthermore, during a period of fasting, daily meals were to be reduced in number from two to one, although this churchly recommendation was also often disregarded.

Alongside the rules on fasting, the medieval Church stressed the importance of moderation with regard to food and drink, condemning excessiveness. Immoderation was a sin (gluttony or *gula*, the last of the Seven Deadly Sins) that easily led to other transgressions, sins and crimes. Gluttons were made fearful with threats of damnation and the punishments awaiting them in Hell, where they could expect torture from a relentless, unbearable hunger that found no relief from the decaying, disgusting dishes that devils would force upon them. Theologians promised

the devout that redemption would ultimately release the fallen from all feelings of hunger in Heaven. Notwithstanding, both rich and poor succumbed to overeating, laypeople and clergy alike. Even beggar monks, who had taken the vow of poverty, were commonly accused of being veritable greedy-guts. The French poet, thief and vagabond François Villon (1431–?), for example, ridiculed monks' predilection for the good things of the table in his *Testament*, a collection of poems, by bequeathing capons, puddings and other fatty treats to the good brethren in jest.

You Are What You Eat: Food and Well-being

In medieval times the study of medicine and the consumption of food were closely interrelated, and medical viewpoints had a considerable influence on what people ate and how they prepared their food. Contrary to what is often

15 The gluttonous are fed revolting food in Hell in a 15th-century woodcut from the *Compost et Kalendrier des Bergiers*.

assumed today, back then, too, large numbers of the aristocracy and privileged classes were extremely keen on looking after their health, attempting a richly varied diet, avoiding excesses and drinking alcohol in moderation, well aware of the damage overindulgence could cause. In the fifteenth century six physicians supervised the diet of the Duke of Burgundy. The English *Forme of Cury*, a late fourteenth-century compilation of recipes, was put together by the master chefs at the court of Richard II in collaboration with the royal physicians.

Alongside the Christian approach to health care, the ancient principles of the Greek-born physician Galen of Pergamon (AD 129–c. 200) dominated medical thinking in the Middle Ages. According to Galen's theories on the cardinal humours or the study of fluids, the components and chief fluids of the human body were blood, phlegm, yellow bile and black bile. Studies on the temperament linked to the theories on the humours divided the former into four groups: sanguine, phlegmatic, choleric and melancholy. Warm and moist components came together in the sanguine (air and the essence of spring); hot and dry in the choleric (fire and summer); cold and dry in the melancholy (earth and autumn); and cold and dank in the phlegmatic (water and winter).

Poor health was caused by an imbalance generated by certain changes in the human body's basic components and fluids. These altered according to the seasons or a person's age. The treatment of an illness focused on restoring the balance of the cardinal humours in a patient. The course of the Middle Ages also saw the influence of astrology increase on the theories of medicine, along with an understanding of the effect that the stars had on the balance of the bodily fluids. The curing of diseases could be expedited by selecting, from a celestial perspective, the most auspicious remedies at the prevailing point in time.

Bloodletting, cupping, induced vomiting and sweating were all methods used in the treatment of ailments, alongside administering medication and prescribing a suitable diet. When diagnosing the complaint and deciding on the appropriate care of a patient, physicians took into consideration not only the patient's physical fitness and digestive functions, but the time of year, the quality of the air and the patient's sleeping patterns, bathing habits, physical exercise programme and sexual life. According to the *Kalender of Shepherdes*, the signs of good health were a hearty appetite and a good digestion, good humour, the ability to sleep well, an easy feeling and a light step, being of an average weight (not too fat and not too thin), a healthy-looking complexion and keen senses. The signs of poor health were the opposite.

In the event that a person fell ill, his doctor would venture a guess that something had disturbed the balance of his cardinal humours and natural temperament. The re-establishment of the balance was therefore the central objective of the course of treatment, in which food played an important role. An illness could be cured by ingesting certain substances with contrasting qualities to the particular fluid that had initially caused the problem. If the affliction was brought on by, for instance, exaggerated sanguineness (an excess of blood), the patient was advised to eat generous amounts of moist fish. Many medieval

16 Sobriety and Gluttony depicted in a French manuscript (*c.* 1290–1300). Medieval Christians prepared themselves for the prolonged period of fasting during Lent by celebrating Carnival on Shrove Tuesday, the day before Ash Wednesday. Throughout Carnival Week a 'state of war' prevailed between the supporters of Carnival (hams, sausages and cheeses armed with kitchen utensils) and the champions of Lent (fish and vegetables). The battle between Carnival and Lent was a celebrated literary topic throughout Europe.

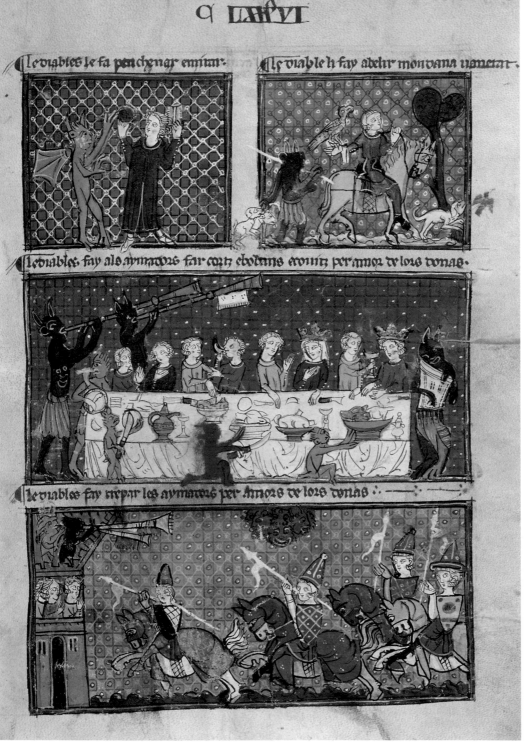

17 Diabolic temptations by personal adornment (top left), by wordly vanities (top right: hunting and hawking), by banquets (centre) and by tournaments (bottom) in *Le Breviari d'amor* by Matfre Ermengau, early 14th century.

recipe collections included separate sections of dishes suitable for the ailing. In general the food given to the infirm had to be nutritious, reasonably warm and reasonably moist. Porridge and gruel made with almond milk were recommended, and also chicken bouillon, chicken and partridge dishes, pomegranate wine, pike broth, figs, currants and sugar.

In order to nurture the good health of an individual, a doctor might also put together a daily menu selection for the different times of the year, suited to the person's temperament. In other words, dietetics was also a preventive discipline. It was generally believed that certain foods were appropriate for the aristocracy and the rich, who led a stationary life. The digestive system of an aristocrat was noble and refined; therefore, the food he ate did not need to be particularly nutritious, and should not be hard to digest. Foods that sustained the body without making it heavy, or without clouding the mind, were suitable. Delicate birds such as partridges, pheasants, chickens and capons were particularly recommended, as were venison, elk and hare. Beef, goat, salted pork, boar and beans, on the other hand, were better suited to sturdy and strong working-class people such as peasants and manual labourers. They were advised to eat heavy meats or other coarse foods, pepper and dark bread, which were hard to digest but kept up the strength required for work.

Age, too, was important. Small children had to beware of a diet too rich in fish, since it might make them phlegmatic. Veal and beef and partridge broth were recommended. To drink with their meal, children could have boiled water, sweetened with sugar and mixed with wine in a ratio of five parts to one. Children had to be taught self-restraint from an early age. In general medical experts underscored the need to curb an individual's natural appetite, emphasizing the importance of eating and drinking in moderation. People were advised to get up from the table before they were fully satisfied. Indiscriminate eating damaged a person's brains, sight and hearing, and obstructed the digestive process, giving rise to strong fluids and causing heaviness, bloating, sleepiness and inertia, as well as weakening the limbs and stomach.

With regard to daily eating patterns, regularity was to everyone's advantage. According to the instructions issued by the Salerno Medical School, in order to live a long life, a person should rise at five o'clock in the morning, have dinner at nine, supper at five and go to bed at nine o'clock in the evening (*Surge quinta, prande nona, Coena quinta, dormi nona, Nec est morti vita prona.*).

The learned were of the general opinion that eating should be conducted only twice daily, and not until the previous meal had been fully digested; anything else was dangerous. Nor was it advisable to eat late. Some scientists recommended only dinner to be served warm, while supper was to be kept rather frugal and easily digestible. This was important particularly with regard to melancholies, whose ailments worsened from the weight of food and the humidity of night time.

Healthy adults should furthermore avoid eating between meals. Exceptions could be made for children, youth, the elderly and the infirm, who needed the sustenance that nutritious foods provided. A young body was better nurtured with frequent meals than with meals that were few and far between, and too heavy.

Seasonal Health Guidelines

The seasons affected people's diets in two ways in the Middle Ages: the availability of specific food items waxed and waned, and medical science linked foods to their rightful season. A cautious individual would avoid all substances whose humoral properties might aggravate the temperament distinctive to the season, rather than allowing nutrition to help the body to withstand the seasonal dangers. The directives from medical experts differed to a certain degree. According to some it was not advisable to eat lentils or anything sweet in March, root vegetables in April, leafy lettuces in June, anything that heated the blood or gave rise to black bile in August, and cabbage in December. Health guides comprised lists of foods to steer clear of, as well as directories on what was safe to eat in the different seasons.

The fourth section of the popular *Kalender of Shepherdes* concluded with a guide to healthy living adapted to the different seasons. It advised people to dress warmly enough between the months of March and May, although not too warmly. Spring was an opportune time for bloodletting in order to remove bad bodily fluids. Light, reinvigorating meats such as chicken or kid in a verjus sauce, soft-boiled eggs, pike and perch were appropriate fare. Wine that was neither too full-bodied nor too light was permitted. People were encouraged to sleep late in the mornings; however, naps were not to be taken during the day. Nor was one to gorge oneself on food. All meat and fish were to be roasted rather than boiled. The instructions for spring in the German-language *Provenzalische Diätetik*

were of a similar nature, recommending plump quail, partridge, goat's milk and green salad.

According to the *Kalender of Shepherdes*, people ought to dress in cool and light clothing, preferably linen, in the months of June, July and August. Light and reinvigorating meat and fish dishes were permitted, such as chicken in an acidic verjus sauce – just like in spring – and young rabbits, salads, melon, lemon, pears and plums. Portions should be small, though frequent, and overly salty foods were to be avoided. Fresh, boiled water sweetened with sugar (*ptizaine*) should be taken frequently in addition to other cooling waters and light wine diluted with one-third water. Strenuous work and overexertion were cautioned against, and sexual intercourse was to be abstained from altogether; frequent concold-water baths were strongly recommended. In the mornings the hands, mouth and face should be washed with refreshing water. The *Provenzalische Diätetik* confirmed that summer called for foods appropriate to hot and dry weather, suggesting pomegranates, sour apples,

18 Astrology influenced medical beliefs and therefore also dietary recommendations. Those born under the sign of Venus (Taureans and Librans) were considered prone to linger long around the pleasures of the dining table, chatting, eating and drinking good wine.

19 A potion is prepared for a bed-bound patient in an illustration from a medieval manuscript. In the Nordic countries views on health issues similar to those in southern Europe were supported. In his prayer book *Rucouskiria Bibliasta*, the Finnish clergyman and 'father of the Finnish written language' Mikael Agricola (c. 1510–1557) included some practical information on astrology, wholesome living and the weather, in addition to prayers pertaining to different situations in life. In the calendar section the months of the year and the most important annual celebrations were listed, each month featuring a poem about matters of current interest. For September Agricola recommended bread with goat's or sheep's milk, and suggested the benefit of cupping and bloodletting, or the removal of bad blood. Vegetables and fruits such as apples and pears were to be consumed, as well as nettle juice. In October boiled pork was good to eat, as was poultry and wildfowl. People were advised to drink young wine, goat's or sheep's milk and beverages seasoned with pepper and cloves. In November mustard, pepper, agrimony (*Agrimonia eupatoria*, a plant of the rose family) and onions were fit for consumption.

cucumbers and squashes, and veal, kid or some other light meat in an acidic sauce.

Between the months of September and November the *Kalender of Shepherdes* advised people to dress the way they did in the spring, although in slightly warmer fabrics. Again, it was a propitious time for bloodletting and ridding the body of bad fluids. Autumn was the most disease-ridden time of the year; therefore choice meats such as capon, chicken and young pigeon should be consumed, washed down with a good wine in moderation. Fresh fruit was cautioned against in order to avoid dangerous fevers. The saying was that he who never eats fruit, never comes down with a fever (*Et dient que celluy neut onques fievres qui onques ne mangu de fruictz*). Water should not be ingested at all, nor should people use cold water to wash any body parts apart from the face and hands. At night the head had to be protected from cold – in other words, a nightcap ought to be worn. People were not to stay in bed and sleep until high noon, although they should take care not to work too hard, or to get exceedingly hungry or thirsty. The *Provenzalische Diätetik*, again, put great stress on the need for warm and moist foods in the autumn, when the weather was cold and dry. It also listed certain fruits such as ripe grapes and wine-soaked figs. For meat, mature, two-year-old mutton, chicken and wildfowl in ginger or saffron sauce were recommended.

In December, January and February the *Kalender of Shepherdes* advised people to wear thick, woollen clothes and furs, particularly fox, whose coat was the warmest. Beef, pork and venison, and all other types of game as well as hazel grouse, pheasant, hare and river birds,

20 A choleric, a sanguine, a melancholy and a phlegmatic: temperament types as pictured in a 15th-century woodcut.

were to be consumed, together with full-bodied wines. All meat should be seasoned with fine spices. Winter was the time of the year when people were at their very healthiest and only fell ill from overindulgent lifestyles. In order to help the body to endure the cold and damp winter season, the *Provenzalische Diätetik* counselled people to eat, first and foremost, roasted meat and meat pies seasoned with pepper and other spices, washed down with generous amounts of wine, either plain or spiced.

Food Products and Medicine

The principles of the cardinal humours extended to food products and food preparation as well, determining what took place in the kitchens. Medieval scholars maintained that everything in existence was a combination of two pairs of elements that affected the temperaments: hot and cold, and dry and moist.

All food products had their given temperament, and the temperament of what a person ate affected his own temperament. The most beneficial and risk-free foods were those whose distinctive properties most closely resembled the individual's own distinctive properties when in a normal, healthy state. Hence the Milanese physician Maino de Maineri, for instance, devoted a large section of the pages in his health guide *Regimen sanitatis* (c. 1330), which he dedicated to his benefactor the Bishop of Arras, to the natural properties of food products.

In the kitchen the choice of cooking method was often influenced by the intention to correct the humour of the food at hand, which might be harmful to the person eating it. Owing in some degree to the prevailing viewpoints on health, the medieval kitchen featured a great number of sauces, for the more prominent the undesirable properties in certain food products were, the more thoroughly were offsetting ingredients used to blend and bind them. Among cooking techniques, boiling was known to heat, but also to moisten. Beef, which was a relatively dry product, should for that very reason be boiled or braised rather than, for instance, roasted. Roasting dried and heated the food and was therefore the best possible method for cooking pork, which was particularly moist, and certain waterfowl, which were cool and moist by nature.

The ideal cooking methods for meat of a moderate temperament were frying, deep-frying or baking inside a pastry shell, the latter creating an element of hot air. These methods heated as well as dried the product to a certain extent. Pastry protected food products with only moderately moist distinctive properties, such as veal, chicken and certain wildfowl. Adding cubes of lard to the dough also helped to preserve the natural moisture of the meat in question.

According to the experts, the preparation of fish required particularly great care. The best and safest specimens were those that resembled land animals: harbour porpoises, sharks, dolphins and codfish. Since fish generally had moist and cold distinctive properties, they were often grilled or fried and served with a compatible sauce containing warm and dry herbs and spices, which neutralized any harmful properties.

Derived from the earth, vegetables often had dry distinctive properties. Boiling or steaming gave them their required moisture. Most grains were moderately cool and dry and therefore suitable for porridge. Wheat was a relatively warm and dry cereal, well suited to a number of purposes. Melons, squashes and cucumbers were cold and moist and believed to cause stomach decay and fever if not handled correctly. Perilously moist vegetables of the onion family were often fried, since frying removed their harmful moisture. Fruits, too, generally had moist distinctive properties, and were therefore commonly roasted, baked inside a pastry shell or combined with ingredients of a dry nature. Some medical experts deemed raw pears to be downright poisonous and only to be consumed together with a warming wine, even after they had been poached.

On the whole, spices enjoyed predominantly hot and dry properties. Several herbs, as well as *aqua vitae*, were known first and foremost as medicine. The inclusion of sugar in a variety of dishes was also warranted, as sugar was an extremely warm and moist commodity, and was considered one of the safest food products.

21 A banquet at the court of King Ahaseurus of Persia, in a 15th-century tapestry from a set depicting the story of Esther.

22 In this picture from a Flemish calendar reapers break for a bite to eat. The sickle is a harvesting tool that has been used since prehistoric times. Well suited to use by women in particular, it came to be a popular wedding present for a farmer's bride.

two

OUR DAILY BREAD

Grain products constituted the staple food of the Europeans in the Middle Ages. Grain provided common people with almost all of their daily nutritional needs – up to 90 per cent – and was eaten at every meal in one form or another. From the eleventh century onwards the cultivation of wheat was widespread throughout Europe, with the exception of the Nordic countries. Spelt, a type of wheat originating in the Near East, was also widely grown. The German abbess and healer Hildegard of Bingen (1098–1179), among others, spoke highly of its wholesome and beneficial qualities. Other common types of food grain were rye and barley, the latter also a key ingredient in the brewing of beer. Both were important export products in the Baltic region. Oats had been cultivated along the Mediterranean Sea since around the first century. They could grow in arid soil, and were raised primarily for animal fodder. To some extent they were grown for human consumption, too, milled into flour or crushed into groats.

Millet was grown quite extensively in, for instance, northern Italy. Buckwheat was a fifteenth-century novelty that only rarely made it onto the tables of the upper classes. Rice had found its way to Europe in the fourth century

BC; however, not until the fifteenth century did rice cultivation get under way in Italy and Spain, where it turned out to be of good quality and relatively inexpensive to boot. By the end of the Middle Ages rice was also imported to the Baltic region. Medieval medical science rated rice very highly, and it was food for the elite. It was also ground into flour and used as a thickening agent.

Pease Porridge Hot, Pease Porridge Cold

Hot cereals considered good enough for the tables of the upper classes included thick porridges made from hulled seeds, groats and coarsely ground grains cooked in beef stock or milk, or almond milk on days of fasting. Eggs, cheese and spices could be added to the dish. Among the most common hot cereals was frumenty: hulled wheat boiled in milk and seasoned with cinnamon and sugar (*fromentiera* in Italian, *fourmentée* in French), an accompaniment well suited to mutton and game such as elk, boar and hare. Millet and rice prepared in the same manner were also worthy complements at even the most sophisticated of tables. The rice could be tinted with saffron for a beautiful yellow colour.

The lower classes ate much porridge and gruel. In the Nordic countries porridge made from

23 In the North barley and rye were predominantly cultivated in the Middle Ages, although wheat and oats also filled the fields. The crops were harvested earlier than is customary nowadays, so the seeds would not drop to the ground. Several different types of grain could be cultivated in the same field. In the Nordic countries grain crops were harvested twice a year in medieval times; accordingly the fields were seeded in the spring as well as in the autumn. As a rule the grain sown in the autumn was gathered by the end of July, and the spring grain by early August.

24 Two women preparing pasta from wheat flour in a late 14th-century manuscript illustration.

water and coarse-ground flour was everyday fare for common people. Other ancient, flour-based foods particular to the remote households of the northern wilderness were *pepu* and *mutti*. *Pepu* was usually rye flour stirred into cold water or fish stock; in *mutti*, the flour was boiled in the liquid. *Mutti* was also a substitute for bread. When venturing into the wilderness or going off to battle, the warriors of the North carried with them nothing but ground grains to eat. The food stores on-board Viking ships consisted primarily of flour and butter, since porridge was the most important cooked food. In the Nordic countries rye flour was also sweetened and made into a paste (*vari*) that could be enjoyed combined with water.

25 Returning from a hunt, depicted in a Flemish calendar. In the background grain is being threshed. The gathered grain was initially dried in the fields, and then desiccated further inside a drying barn. For the outdoor drying process, the grain stalks were tied into sheaves that were either arranged in stooks in the field or grouped together in shocks of several sheaves, each propped upright and supporting one another. On top of each shock, a separate sheaf was placed, capping the structure. Once dried, the grain was threshed and the seeds were taken to the mill. The oldest type of watermill, the pestle or stamping mill, had been used in the North since late prehistoric times. In Central Europe both mills and baking ovens were taken into use even earlier, an indication that bread was eaten more commonly than porridge on the Continent.

Dishes containing flour were put together for the tables of the upper classes as well. In Italy, for instance, flour soup was prepared by adding wheat flour to sweetened water, beef stock or soft curd. Mature cheese, spices, sugar and rose water were sprinkled on top. Already in medieval times, pasta dough was made from wheat flour, although pasta was still far from being considered the national dish of Italy. Different types of pasta were made by hand in private kitchens; yet Florence, for one, was already in the late Middle Ages home to a lasagne-makers' guild. Vermicelli, macaroni and other pasta shapes as well as filled ravioli were familiar varieties at the time. Pasta was served with cheese, butter and spices – neither tomato sauce nor tomatoes, for that matter, were known yet. Broken pieces of macaroni were also made use of in soups. Ravioli was prepared in the same way as today: filled with a mixture of cheese and meat or eggs. Pasta was primarily perceived as food for the poor. By colouring the dough with saffron, some panache was added to pasta dishes for the upper classes, while almond milk, sugar and rose water created the base for a sumptuous filling.

Pies and Bakery Products

Besides bread, sweet or savoury pies and a variety of other bakery products, such as wafers, were also made from flour. As with pasta dough, there were two principal types of pie dough: a simple version consisting mainly of flour, water and salt, and a more elaborate variety including eggs and optionally also saffron, sugar or rose water. Already in medieval times, folded pastry cases similar to Cornish pasties were prepared. These were filled with vegetables, meat or fish, and were typical also in eastern Finland, where they were called 'roosters' (*kukko*).

Bread was an essential element of mealtimes among the common people, as were porridges and gruels. Similarly, bread was always at hand at the tables of the upper classes, although mostly as a supplement. When the wealthy sat down to eat, bread tended to function as a gauge of social standing: the host and his guests of honour were given larger helpings than the other diners. Generally the host's pieces were fresh, while those of his guests of honour could be a day old, and those of the other diners older still.

The wealthy would have nothing but pure, white wheat bread with their meals, as doctors recommended. The husks were removed from the grains, and the kernels milled into fine flour. Dark bread made from rye, barley, oat, millet or mixed flour, the latter often a blend of rye and wheat called *meslin* or *maslin*, belonged especially to the lower classes of society, although in many places towards the end of the Middle Ages, the common people, too, began to favour light wheaten bread. In France, Italy and England bread soup was also a well-known dish, made from vegetable stock or seasoned water poured over sliced bread. A more elaborate version could be created by adding saffron, almonds, spices and wine or beer to the mixture.

At mealtimes in the Middle Ages flat rounds or slices of bread also served as trenchers, off which pieces of meat, thick sauces and food in general were eaten. Ultimately these trencher breads (*taillor* or *tranchoir* in French) were also

St Anthony's Fire, or Ergotism

Central Europe was in the Middle Ages ravaged by a potentially deadly disease that escalated into wide-reaching epidemics, the source of which was unknown. Later it came to be referred to as St Anthony's Fire or ergotism. According to Bishop Gregory of Tours (c. AD 538-594), author of the *History of the Franks* (*Historia francorum*), the disease had already appeared in France in 591. The onset of the illness manifested itself in burning sensations and rashes on the extremities, which blackened and ultimately became gangrenous. Other symptoms included chest cramps, muscle cramps, disorientation and unconsciousness. We know for a fact that ergotism claimed roughly 40,000 lives in the German regions north of the Rhine in the year 994, and some 14,000 in 1129.

In 1089 the French nobleman Gaston Guérin founded the Order of Saint-Didier de la Mothe, an organization of laypeople who cared for those that had fallen victim to the disease. Guérin's own son is said to have recovered from the illness with the help of the hallowed remains of St Anthony, also known as Anthony of Egypt or Anthony the Great. For this reason St Anthony was declared the patron saint of the order, whose members were accordingly called Antonians. St Anthony also became the protector of all those who suffered from this disease, and the disease itself came to be called St Anthony's Fire.

St Anthony's Fire was treated by feeding white bread and pork to the afflicted. In the visual arts of the era St Anthony was commonly depicted holding a T-cross, with a piece of bread in one hand and a pig at his feet. The animal wore a bell around its neck; consequently the pigs raised by the Antonians were also fitted with bells to distinguish them from other pigs in the area. Even in faraway Finland St Anthony was worshipped as the protector of pigs and a deliverer from plagues.

Mikael Agricola mentions him in his prayer book from 1544, and the saint himself was by tradition called Tynimys or Kynänen, terms of endearment derived from Anthony or Antoninus.

The French physician Thuillier of the medical centre in Angers suggested in 1670 that the symptoms of St Anthony's Fire were caused by ergot, a fungal disease of rye, and that the affliction itself was not contagious in humans. However it was not until 1746 that the Medical Academy of Paris accepted this theory. Certain alkaloids present in contaminated rye precipitate the disease by causing the veins and arteries in humans to contract dramatically. Symptoms appear if as little as 8.1 per cent of the ingested rye contains ergot, and in any rainy year in the Middle Ages the amount of contaminated grain could have increased a hundredfold. Ergot proved dangerous to livestock as well: abortions and stillbirths were seen in cattle that were pastured in rye fields after the harvest.

In addition to the gangrene-causing *ergotismus gangraenosus*, cases of *ergotismus convulsivus*, a condition that manifested itself foremost as a disorder of the nervous system, were also noted. This disease began by a prickling sensation in the fingertips, followed by numbness, and progressed into muscle cramps and epileptic convulsions. Another common symptom was miscarriage. In children the disease stunted mental development.

Ergot was less prevalent in cooler climates, although it caused hardship in the Nordic countries during the modern period: in Sweden from the 1740s onwards and in Finland a century later. Due to the muscle cramps associated with the disease, it was referred to as 'the wrenching sickness'. To date archaeological research has also unveiled the presence of ergot in certain Finnish counties (Hämeenlinna, Lieto and Kastelholma) in the Middle Ages.

26 Flat rounds of bread serve as trenchers in a painting by the Master of the Housebook.

27 A burgher's wife brings bread to be baked in the town's communal oven. Medieval ovens were simple, cavernous stone structures.

consumed, or given to the poor or to animals. Stale crusts and heels of bread were not disposed of, but soaked and softened in soups. And, as previously mentioned, the centre of the bread was also used in cooking as a binding agent for sauces.

At table bread was generally served as food, although it could, as discussed, double as a plate, or a spoon, saltcellar or finger wipe. Easy to handle and absorbent, flat pieces of bread worked well as trenchers, cut from loaves that were a few days old and made from coarse-ground meal. On formal occasions the ordinary diner sliced his bread himself, while guests of honour were given theirs ready-sliced. The latter

were also likely to have their trencher breads changed several times during the course of the meal. As a rule lowlier diners received a new piece at least for the last course. Ultimately the bread was used to soak up sauces, or given to the dogs to eat, or to the poor as alms. In the late Middle Ages the usage of trencher breads was more common in northern Europe than in the South.

In towns and villages bread-baking was principally assigned to professional bakers, in part to reduce the risk of fire. Not even all wealthy, aristocratic households baked their bread at home in their own ovens. Towns and villages provided entrepreneurial oven owners who kept

28 December in a Flemish calendar: a pig is slaughtered and bread is baked in the oven.

their ovens burning for communal use. Dough could be prepared at home and taken to the public oven for baking. If bread was bought already baked, the type of flour used determined the price, light wheat bread being the most expensive. The loaves were usually round.

Today there remain disappointingly few bread recipes from the Middle Ages, a fact that may seem odd in view of the central role bread played at mealtimes and in the daily diet of people. At the time bread-baking was one of life's basic skills, and the recording of recipes was therefore not deemed necessary. However, since bread was an integral part of daily eating, this book does include a selection of bread recipes. These recipes have been worked out based on the information available to us today.

GRAIN: FRUIT OF THE EARTH

Grain, more than anything else, has been the quintessential symbol of the fruits of the earth. The progress of grain from field to dough and onwards to oven and table has been equated with the different stages of human life. Buried in the ground, the seed appears dead, only to sprout again in the spring. It was therefore the perfect allegory of rebirth and hope.

Grain appears in numerous Bible stories. It appears in the passages about the sacrificial offerings of Cain and Abel (Genesis 4:1–17). It is there in the dreams of Joseph (Genesis 37:5–8), in the dreams of Pharaoh (Genesis 41:1–31) and in the Book of Ruth (Book 3). In the Old Testament the Offerings for the Sanctuary (Exodus 25-30) were the symbols of spiritual sustenance. In the New Testament the parable of the Miracle of the Loaves and Fishes mentions twelve basketfuls of the product left over from the five loaves and two fish, with which Jesus fed the masses (Matthew 14:17–21). Man shall not live by bread alone (Matthew 4:3–4); man needs spiritual food as well. During the Last Supper, the bread of life, along with wine, became food for the soul. 'While they were eating, Jesus took bread, and when he had given thanks, he broke it and gave it to his disciples, saying: Take and eat; this is my body. (Matthew 26:26. See also Mark 14:22, Luke 22:19; John 12:24.)

The ears of grain portrayed in some medieval paintings of the Virgin Mary and the Infant Jesus made direct reference to the Last Supper. In certain German nunneries and in pilgrim iconography from the fourteenth century onwards, the Virgin Mary was pictured 'dressed in grain' – in other words, her cloak was adorned with the seed-bearing heads of cereal plants. The subject-matter stemmed from the *Song of Songs* (Song of Solomon 7:2), in which 'your waist is a mound of wheat, encircled by lilies'. Mary was the sacred field that, un-seeded, bore the grain that was the Christ Child, the bread of life. In popular piety Mary, clad in ears of grain, was invoked in the springtime prayers in the fields for the safeguarding of a good harvest. In the ancient past Demeter, the Greek goddess of agriculture and the 'mother of grain', had been a similar character. Her Roman equivalent was Ceres. In medieval Finland, too, field-blessing weeks (*kanttaiviikko*) were celebrated in the spring, during which villagers, led by their parish priest, made their way to the fields in a ceremonial procession to pray for a good harvest. ◁

29 A nobleman's garden in a Flemish illustration for the *Roman de la rose*. The left side has turf and a fountain, while the right contains beds of herbs; both are shaded by fruit trees. In his *Dictionarius* (*c.* 1220) John of Garland, an English-born grammarian and teacher at the University of Paris, provided a detailed inventory of what a well-planted Paris garden ought to grow. He lists cherry, pear, apple, plum, quince, peach, nut and fig trees as well as grapevines; sage, parsley, hyssop, fennel and chervil; rose, lily and violet; medicinal plants such as mallow, belladonna and sunflower; and vegetables such as cabbages, leeks, garlic and mustard.

three

VEGETABLES FOR ALL
OCCASIONS

In the Middle Ages vegetables and other food plants – including grain – played an essential role in the daily fare of the lower classes. By comparison, the more affluent members of society consumed fewer greens, since they were able to get hold of ample amounts of meat for their tables. Nevertheless, owing to the rules on fasting, food plants were highly useful agricultural products in each and every kitchen.

Vegetables could be eaten raw, although most of the time they were cooked and served in a rather simple, uncomplicated fashion. Thorough rinsing and in many cases also parboiling preceded the actual cooking of the vegetable. Soups in particular were prepared from vegetables, although purées, stews and various vegetable pots were popular as well. Roots and vegetables could also be pan-fried or baked in hot ashes, which gave them a pleasant flavour. Vegetables were not considered particularly nutritious, for which reason it was preferred to boost them with meat and fish. Beef or fish stock could be used as cooking liquid, or almond milk on days of fasting.

The range of vegetables was somewhat more limited in the Middle Ages than today, since potatoes, aubergines, Jerusalem artichokes, tomatoes, maize, sweet peppers, sweet potatoes and green beans were yet to find their way to the tables of Europe in the wake of the great explorers. On the other hand, some species that have since lost their significance, such as turnips and nettles, were commonly consumed.

Many plant species were less successful in northern climates than further south, but the Hanseatic League promoted the availability and use of vegetables in the North as well. During the course of the Middle Ages the peoples of Central and Northern Europe became acquainted with numerous new types of plants that had initially grown in the Mediterranean region, such as cauliflowers, leeks, lettuces and peas. The cultivation of rhubarb was also adopted from Southern Europe, where the plant had arrived in the fourteenth century from Asia. Initially monks grew rhubarb in monastery gardens, and it was bought at great expense for its stimulating effects on the digestive system. A purgative potion or laxative (*purgats*) could be produced from the rhubarb root, mentioned, for instance, in Mikael Agricola's book of prayers (*Rucouskiria*, 1544). Otherwise rhubarb was not really used as a food plant in the Middle Ages, nor was its present-day variety known at the

30 Green vegetables are steamed, chopped and crushed in a mortar in a 14th-century illustration from the *Luttrell Psalter*. Northern peasants made stews mainly from turnips, cabbages, broad beans and onions. Swedes, cabbages and peas were established in Finland in the 15th century, and 16th-century account books from Turku and Häme Castles list beans, peas, cabbages, onions and turnips, while artichokes, parsnips, Brussels sprouts, red onions, pumpkins, fennel, Savoy cabbages, beetroots and radishes were grown in the castle gardens. Only in the 17th century did novelties such as carrots, cucumbers, garden beans, garden peas, spinach, lettuce, leeks and endives arrive in Finland.

time, since it is a later hybrid of which only the leaf stalks are eaten.

Roots and Shoots

In the Middle Ages the categorizing of vegetables and other food plants was different from today. Food plants were often grouped into 'dry' and 'fresh' varieties. The fresh ones, in turn, were divided into roots and herbs. Anything that grew beneath the ground belonged to the root category, therefore foods such as turnips and parsnips were included. 'Herbs' comprised everything that grew above the ground, so lettuce, cress, parsley, cucumbers, cabbages, leeks and onions were considered herbs.

Onions, beans and cabbages enjoyed a special place in everyday food preparation. Savoy cabbage, kale and cauliflower, for instance, had been known in ancient Rome, having been brought back by the conquering legions as bounty from the East. Cabbages were exceptionally hardy, and readily available during the better part of the year in the late Middle Ages. Yet despite being widely cultivated, cabbages were still relatively expensive. England, suffering from an inclement climate, supplemented its cabbage stores with produce from France and Holland, as it did its other vegetable reserves. The early ninth-century grounds of Charlemagne in Aix-la-Chapelle were famous for their vegetable gardens. Charlemagne himself valued green cabbage in particular and, being a great believer in improvement, he developed methods for cultivating 74 different types of vegetables, herbs and fruit.

Kohlrabi and Brussels sprouts were developed in late-medieval Flanders, while broccoli evolved from the wild cabbage that grew in the Mediterranean region. Broccoli was cultivated in southern Europe centuries before it became known in the Nordic countries.

Cabbage and bean soups constituted the main dishes of the common people. Lard and meat were added to the stock to enhance the flavour and fat content. The *Ménagier de Paris* (1393) points out that beef or mutton stock is better suited to cabbage than pork stock, which in turn is excellent with leeks. Only the pale parts of cabbages met with the approval of the upper classes, and it was the same for leeks and lettuces.

Various types of onion plants were also readily available, since they grew well in humble circumstances. Onions were relatively inexpensive, and all social classes used them in food preparation. The bulbs could, for instance, form the main ingredient in a soup, or they could simply serve as an aromatic herb. Chopped onions were generally sautéed in oil before being added to a dish, although it was possible to add raw onions to a soup. Sautéed onions were also used to garnish already cooked dishes. Onions and leeks could also be baked in hot ashes, producing a soft and aromatic final product. If baked the onions were either eaten as they were or used in other food preparation.

According to certain learned opinion, the dangerously moist onion was not to be included in the dishes of the infirm. Yet the onion was believed to possess healing properties as well,

and in the Middle Ages people used potions made from onions in the treatment of afflictions such as digestive disorders, common colds, impotence and oedema. The smell of onions was also believed to drive away vampires. Onions cropped up in many old sayings: a weeping person, for instance, was said to be peeling onions.

By quantity, 'dry vegetables', such as broad beans or field beans, peas and lentils, were the most consumed in the Middle Ages, when they enjoyed an indisputably more important role in everyday eating than they do today. When dried, pulses lasted well throughout the winter, too. The wealthy looked down on lentils, as these were considered poor-man's fare. Bean soups, bean stews, bean pots or mashed beans made up the daily sustenance of the lower classes in particular. Before cooking the beans were soaked, and other low-cost vegetables such as cabbages, leeks and onions could be added to the dish. Pulses could also be added to bread dough, particularly in times when grain was scarce.

The bean and pea dishes of the upper classes were no simple concoctions, but rich and filling stews and mashes. In Italy beans were stuffed: the seeds were soaked, split, stuffed with an almond and sugar paste, and baked. In England beans boiled in almond milk with wine, raisins and honey made a fine delicacy for the tables of the upper classes. Peas, too, could be turned into tantalizing dishes with the help of almond milk and rice flour.

Roots remained in season longer than vegetables, since their growing season was longer. Various root vegetables were used in food preparation in a number of ways, despite medieval medical science warning against roots

Vegetarianism in the Middle Ages

The first known vegetarian in the West was the Greek mathematician and philosopher Pythagoras of Samos (572–497 BC), whose vegetarian mores were founded on principles of ethics. However, these Pythagorean views did not gain much support in late antiquity or the Middle Ages.

In medieval times a diet consisting solely of water and raw, unseasoned vegetables was rare. An uncompromisingly vegetarian diet was admittedly considered a more virtuous way of life – after all, in the Garden of Eden before the Fall man and beast had eaten nothing but plants – although it was hardly ever practised. The medieval Church assured the faithful that the killing of animals for food and nourishment was not a sin. In the thirteenth century the Italian theologian and philosopher Thomas Aquinas asserted in his *Summa Theologica* that God had created plants and animals as food for man. Animals did not possess a rational soul, and therefore did not have the ability to gain knowledge of God, still less entrance into Paradise.

In medieval culture the vegetable kingdom was thought to stand for purity, and was simultaneously seen as the direct opposite of the impure animal kingdom. Even so, the fruits borne by plants were somewhat suspiciously regarded as not being altogether clean, since all fruit ultimately pointed to that one particular event which, at the beginning of time, precipitated the Fall.

It has been suggested that a distinction can be drawn between voluntary vegetarianism and vegetarianism dictated by necessity in the Middle Ages. The poor, who could not afford to eat meat, practised the latter. The members of certain groups viewed as heretics (the Cathars, the Manichaeans, the Bogomils) kept a voluntary vegetarian diet. Among Christians, the most fervent ascetics also maintained a self-imposed vegetarian lifestyle; to mystics and hermits, adhering to vegetarianism was a means of chastising the body and thus achieving divine approval. The Calabrian hermit Francis of Paola, for instance, who lived at the court of King Louis XI of France in the late fifteenth century, was known to be a strict ascetic. For the most part he slept standing or leaning against something. He never cut his hair or beard, nor did he deign to eat meat or fish. As a result the King ordered lemons, sweet oranges, Muscadel pears and parsnips for his hermit. Yet the most famous vegetarian of the fifteenth century was the Italian artist and scientist Leonardo da Vinci, who called the human mouth 'the grave of all animals', and whose notebooks expressed some extremely moving reflections on the fate of slaughterhouse animals.

31 A late 15th-century perception of the Garden of Eden before the Fall, where early man and beast lived entirely on plants. According to present-day archaeological and palaeontological research, the diet of man's forbears – for instance *Homo erectus* – consisted primarily of plants, roots, fruits and nuts, although it was possible for our ancient predecessors to acquire meat as well, either from the carcasses of dead animals or by means of hunting.

being difficult to digest. Turnips were common; carrots, parsnips, beetroots, radishes and horse-radish were also known. Swedes may not have been known until the sixteenth century. In general people at the time liked piquant flavours, and grated horseradish had the same function

as mustard. Horseradish and mooli could be obtained from specialist spice shops, unless grown at home.

Green vegetables eaten in the Middle Ages included celery, fennel, asparagus and spinach, all of which were also put to good use as aromatic

32 Collecting cabbage in the *Tacuinum sanitatis*.

herbs. Asparagus was initially found in the kitchens of the wealthy. Spinach, too, was a newcomer, used particularly on days of fasting. Easy to prepare as an accompaniment to any dish, the spinach was, as per the *Ménagier de Paris*, rinsed and de-stemmed, after which the leaves were pan-fried in oil or boiled in salted water and drizzled with a small amount of olive oil before being served. Spinach is also known to have been included in herbed vegetable pies in the fourteenth century.

Fennel leaves were used in salads, and fennel seeds seasoned drinks, soups, sweets and bread. Medical experts recommended fennel seeds for stomach ache, fever, toothache, earache, tumours and blindness. Fennel was thought to prolong life and promote strength and courage. In the Middle Ages it was used as an antidote to numerous poisons, and it was also believed to cure insanity. Fennel sprigs were hung above the door as a defence against witchcraft, while chewing fennel seeds curbed an excessive appetite.

33 Picking beans in an illustration from a late 14th-century manuscript. Only the seeds of pulses were used in food preparation. Not until the 16th century did the common green bean, whose pods were eaten as well, gain general ground. Bean stew was usually served with pork, although game or goose would also do. The broad bean, native to the Mediterranean region, achieved great popularity due to its almond-like flavour. It arrived in the Nordic countries in the high Middle Ages under the auspices of monks. Peas were similarly well liked, and were freighted and sold throughout Europe in huge quantities. In Finland the pea could be found from the 9th century onwards. The Persians, Greeks and Romans used dried peas in ancient times, but fresh peas did not appear in the kitchens of the West until the 16th century.

Pumpkins, courgettes and cucumbers were all known in the South. When mashed, the yellowish orange pumpkin went well with white meat or fish. In Italy cucumbers were even eaten plain, or seasoned only with salt. Endives, or cultivated leaf chicories, and ordinary lettuces were common leaf vegetables. Lettuce was seasoned with herbs such as parsley, sage, onion, garlic, leeks, borage, mint, fennel, rosemary and rue, and served with a dressing of oil, vinegar and salt mixed together. Cress was also known.

The nettle is nowadays merely a wild plant, whereas in the Middle Ages it was cultivated in kitchen gardens. Nettles were well liked for their mild, slightly bitter and minty flavour. In the medieval kitchen nettles had many incarnations, turning up in purées, soups, stews and bread. The nettle was also an acknowledged medicinal herb. The young leaves were picked, dried and subsequently boiled into a potion beneficial in the treatment of anaemia, rheumatic symptoms, joint ache, dermatological

Dandeaum nobilibus ser. er sapie
re serandum consuetudinem reg
vilumnet age quel decer re agere

rel
dic
bu
par
uo

tae
di f
ta l
suc

terrel aluxre medico. salicce requitand
vuland. Tra tale quid fagen
a bir corpus mulum uwar

conditions and oozing sores, cold symptoms, coughing, rhinitis and inflammation of the bronchial tubes. An aphrodisiac of nettle seeds boiled in wine had been concocted in the first century by the Greek physician, pharmacologist and botanist Dioscorides (*c.* AD 40–*c.* 90), whose volumes on pharmaceutical plants were hugely popular in medieval Europe. (The work is known in English by its Latin title *De materia medica*.) In Finland, in pre-modern times, male impotence was ministered to by whipping the genitalia with whisks of nettles. Various super-ficial stimulation treatments were commonly carried out, the objective being the boosting of the blood circulation and the removal of harmful substances through the skin

The amounts of mushrooms consumed in the Middle Ages are hard to estimate, since wild plants were rarely entered in account books. It is also hard to tell which mushrooms were actually eaten, as exact species are generally not specified in medieval recipes. Some mushroom types were definitely known to be poisonous, and we also know that even then truffles, or earthnuts, were delicacies destined for the wealthy. According to medieval medical experts, mushrooms possessed dangerously moist, distinctive properties and so required special handling. Thorough cleaning and parboiling was of the essence, after which the mushrooms might still be pan-fried and served together with, say, onions or leeks. As today, mushrooms were also dried and stored for use out of season. Dried mushrooms were soaked before being added to stewed or baked preparations.

opposite: 34 At a royal table food and drinks are served from gold and silver vessels, in an edition of the *Secret of Secrets* (*De secretis secretorum*, 1326–7).

In the Medieval Kitchen

In the dwellings of peasants and craftsmen one room served as both kitchen and dining space. Conversely the palaces of the aristocracy and the urban homes of the high bourgeoisie featured a separate kitchen section, while the ceremonial room functioned as a dining area in which tables were assembled at mealtimes. In other words, the dining table was not a stationary piece of furniture. Traditionally all members of the household dined together; however, in the late Middle Ages the custom of dining in smaller, separate dining rooms became more common, at which point the architecture of the houses also changed. Among the upper classes, the lord of the house and his family preferred to take especially breakfast and supper amid a small circle of kin rather than in the company of a large group of people.

In upper-class households the kitchen was not situated next to the dining area but as far as possible from the lounges and living quarters, because of the risk of fire or smoke inhalation. The castle or palace kitchens usually consisted of a suite of rooms accommodating anything from five to fifty workers at a time. Constant exposure to heat and smoke called for the kitchen facilities to be uncrowded and well ventilated.

There was much hustle and bustle in the kitchens of large households, since most dishes were meant to be eaten warm. Only certain pies, jellies, uncooked sauces and food compositions were served cold and could therefore be prepared in advance. At dinnertime the swift serving staff whisked the completed dishes from the kitchen to the dining area. Table linen and crockery were also stored in the kitchen or in an adjacent pantry-cum-storage room, from which they were taken to the dining hall whenever it was time to set the table.

In fifteenth-century Dijon the palace kitchens of the Dukes of Burgundy accommodated six to seven immense fireplaces. They also held several washbasins, in which food products, cooking utensils and receptacles were washed. A skilled head chef — such as Maître Chiquart, who served the Duke of Savoy — would emphasize the importance of cleanliness in his kitchen with a passion bordering on fanaticism. Kitchen waste was a considerable problem in the Middle Ages. If there was a river nearby, the refuse could be discarded there. Otherwise it had to be carted separately to the rubbish heap outside town. The most cavalier housekeepers threw their waste directly into the street for pigs and stray dogs to scavenge — and for passers-by to be plagued by.

As regards cooking vessels and utensils, a cauldron and a cast iron or copper pan were irreplaceable in the inventory of every medieval kitchen. Soups and meat or vegetable stews were prepared in large pots or cauldrons. A pot with a tripod was an indispensable implement when preparing meat, particularly in peasant homes, since the lower classes did not own skewers, gridirons or other appliances used for cooking on an open fire. Large kitchens were also equipped with several frying pans. Long-handled frying pans were common and practical appliances when cooking over an open flame, as they protected the cook from the heat. Upper-class kitchens were furnished with a number of different types of skewers and rotisseries appropriate to their various purposes. Food could also be

roasted on a grill or in a hinged gridiron, the latter being a medieval innovation. Grilling, roasting and rotisserie baking were mostly done in urban homes and the kitchens of the aristocratic minority.

Graters, mortars and pestles were also important kitchen implements. Even meat could be minced in a mortar. Sieves and straining cloths were equally essential, since bread, meat, spices and other ingredients were first ground and then strained through gauze in order to produce smooth, lump-free textures. Ladles were needed for stirring and dishing up soups, and knives for cutting and chopping meat and vegetables.

In the chimneyless cottages and cooking huts of northern Finland people got by with extremely basic equipment, traditionally consisting of a ladle, a *puukko* or all-purpose hunting knife and a mortar, plus the odd cast iron pot or saucepan. Cast iron cauldrons with legs, hinged gridirons and wooden plunger churns, in which larger batches of butter than ever before could be churned in one go, were medieval novelties. Kitchen implements, eating utensils and storage receptacles were made of wood, bone or horn. In peasant cottages warm food was brought to table in the cooking pot; cold dishes were served in bowls or on wooden platters. Diners helped themselves to food with their fingers, although everyone kept his or her personal knife and spoon. Guests and travellers passing by brought along their own spoons and knives.

Upper-class Finnish homes were as well equipped with first-rate cookware and crockery as their Continental counterparts. A fifteenth-century inventory of the estate of Nils Tavast, Hundred Court Judge, in Hollola in southern Finland, lists 22 cauldrons, several rotisseries large enough for roasting the entire carcass of an animal, saucepans (of which one alone was intended for the brewing of beer), jugs, silver goblets, drinking horns, six tablecloths and numerous towels for wiping the hands. When the Polish Princess Catherine Jagellon, wife to Duke John of Finland, arrived at Turku Castle accompanied by her retinue on Christmas Eve 1562, her shipping trunks for the occasion contained, among other things, table linen from Cologne, a yellow Turkish tablecloth with hand towels, 54 silver plates and 91 silver bowls, twelve large lidded and gilded beakers, assorted bottles, bowls, spoons and forks, salt cellars, two jugs and one washbasin. Tin bowls and plates were brought along for everyday use. The cooking implements included two frying pans, four Italian saucepans, a meat cauldron, a pudding pan, an egg pan, a pasty pan, six cake moulds, a serving fork, two colanders, twelve lidded containers, a cake spatula and, last but not least, some tin bottles for oil and vinegar.

35 Pigs, cattle and sheep in Pietro de' Crescenzi's *Le Rustican* (1470). In the Middle Ages domestic animals were smaller than their present-day counterparts. Bovines had shorter legs, while the anatomy of swine was more delicate than today and the shape of a pig's head rather resembled that of a wild boar. Animals were part of the daily life of man, in towns as well as in the countryside. However, efforts were made, through municipal by-laws, to intervene in the unconfined pasturing of livestock, which sometimes resulted in disorder. In certain cities it was the duty of the official hangman to apprehend any runaways. Residents of the city of Turku in southwest Finland kept farmland outside the municipal boundaries. In the morning the city herdsmen took the residents' animals to pasture in one large group, and in the evening the respective owners identified their own beasts by their earmarks.

four

UNDER THE SPELL
OF MEAT

In the late Middle Ages plagues and epidemics reduced the size of the human population to the extent that there was more meat available per capita than previously. Even so, a diet abounding in meat enabled the aristocrats and the wealthy bourgeoisie to demonstrate, in an increasingly forceful fashion, their privileged position in society. By contrast, the framework of fasting dictated by Christianity and the authority of the Church also determined the approach to meat. Particularly objectionable was the excessive consumption of red meat. Moralists strived to influence prevailing social attitudes by associating red meat with unsavoury, disreputable groups of people who were prone to overindulgence. Mercenaries, for instance, were one such lot. Unrestrained consumption of red meat was unquestionably unhealthy, bringing about gout and other ills.

Pork and Capon: All-round Favourites

Great quantities of domestic animal meat were eaten in the Middle Ages: beef, pork, mutton and poultry. Horsemeat, on the other hand, was fairly uncommon fare. The consumption of beef increased towards the end of the Middle Ages; still, pork was the most common type of meat consumed, especially at a normal farmhouse dinner. Preserved pork in particular was used in a variety of dishes, although at slaughtering time fresh pork was also eaten. Pigs fared well in northern climates, too, and as domestic animals were easy to care for, since they generally foraged for food themselves. Pork yielded good-tasting, long-lasting salted meat.

The English upper classes preferred pork, followed by beef, veal and lamb in a fairly evenly balanced succession. In Italy the elite favoured domestic lamb and pork, since beef had to be brought in from abroad. These regional taste differences reflected local production fairly accurately: in England cattle farming was well developed.

In Finland cattle farming was concentrated in the arable areas in the western part of the country, where dung was needed for the fields. The herd of an ordinary Finnish farm in the fifteenth century counted a couple of oxen as draught animals, two to four cows and some half a dozen sheep. Pigs and chickens were not tallied. According to the statistics on cattle tax dating from the early modern period, the cattle-farming counties of Finland were mainly situated

36 An ox, from the *Luttrell Psalter*. The milk and meat derived from cattle has been used as food for thousands of years. The ox was a beast of burden and its flesh was therefore tough. As a result, ox meat was rarely served at upper-class banquets. In the French countryside *Boeuf Gras*, a joyous event celebrating the ox, took place every year on the eve of Lent, when the finest ox in the region was decked out and paraded through town in a festive procession – on the way to slaughter.

along the western and southwestern coasts of the country. Discoveries of farm animal bones in Viljandi County in Livonia, a historic region comprising most of present-day Latvia and Estonia, indicate that primarily beef was being eaten, followed by mutton and goat, pork, chicken and assorted game such as hare, elk and venison. It appears that poultry was reserved especially for the wealthy citizens of Viljandi. Archaeozoological research in the medieval cities of present-day Estonia (Tartu, Tallinn, Pärnu and Haapsalu) has uncovered the remains of primarily cattle, pigs, sheep and goats, which leads us to believe that the good burghers were not very avid huntsmen.

Among domestic fowl, practically all present-day species were known in the Middle Ages, with the exception of the turkey, which did not arrive from the New World until the modern period. Popular domestic species were capons, hens, chickens, ducks and geese. Capons were valued for being larger, fatter and tenderer than regular roosters as a result of the caponizing or castrating process. Wildfowl were also readily available in large households, since game birds were hunted in forests, and pigeons and other species were raised in cotes. Many forest birds were perceived as upper-class fare. The flavour of domestic fowl, too, was often gamier than today, as the birds were left to roam free in search of natural feed.

Large amounts of fowl of assorted feathers were consumed in German monasteries, for example. Goose was considered a great delicacy for its fat content. Seasoned and stuffed with garlic and quince, for instance, it was roasted on a spit. Goose liver was highly cherished in monasteries, especially in France. Fat-laden goose livers were achieved by feeding the birds figs and chestnuts. Ducks were also roasted on monastery rotisseries, stuffed with dried or fresh fruits, or with seasoned pork, breadcrumbs and eggs. Pigeons were used for soups and large pies.

Noble Game

Game was an important product in the medieval food industry. The upper classes held game in very high esteem – particularly red deer and wild boar, hare and rabbit – preferring it to the meat of domestic animals. Red deer were hunted mostly in July and August, when the animals were at their plumpest. The red deer was also an important symbolic creature, to which other deer, such as roe and fallow, were often likened. In Christian iconography a fundamental starting point presented itself in the Book of Psalms (42:2): 'As the hart panteth after the water brooks, so panteth my soul after thee, O God.' The hart's quest for the water brook denoted man's pursuit of purifying baptismal water, and so the image of a deer became a favoured motif in relief on baptismal fonts. The second-century bestiary *Physiologus*, still popular in the Middle Ages, compared deer to ascetics 'who, with their tears of repentance, quell the burning arrows of the Evil One'. In medieval ecclesiastic art the deer nibbling on a grapevine symbolized man, who already in this life may partake of God's mercy. Deer were also thought to possess a number of extraordinary skills such as having the power to suck snakes out of their holes. They could also protect themselves from snake

37 Birds are taken for plucking and cooking. In the cities specialist shops sold poultry. Every peasant kept his own chicken coop, and city dwellers, too, raised domestic fowl, which were easier to feed than other livestock. The poor kept domestic fowl primarily for their eggs. Archaeological research indicates that the citizens of Turku kept numerous hens, in addition to which they had ducks, geese and wildfowl.

venom by drinking spring water for three hours on end, and then continue living for another fifty years. Stags' antlers were believed to contain healing as well as magical powers: burned to ashes, they drove away snakes. The flesh of a deer, again, was said to bring down fever, and a salve made from its bone marrow cured many ills.

The flesh of a wild boar was greatly valued, although hunting the animal proved dangerous.

Full-grown hogs were strong and ferocious beasts, and it was uncertain whether the hunter or the hunted would emerge the victor. Often men, horses and dogs died or were gravely injured in the process. In the Middle Ages the symbolism attached to wild boars was certainly more appealing than the archetype of a domestic pig. The latter was often the epitome of sin, greed and ignorance. One exception was St Anthony's sow, whose fat, according to legend, cured the future saint from disease. In iconography St Anthony's sow also symbolizes his victory over carnal temptations and evil enticements.

In the late Middle Ages game was less readily available, thus becoming, even more potently than before, an entitlement of the upper classes: a testimony to wealth and clout that was emphat-ically demonstrated, particularly on formal occasions. The most commonly consumed game were wildfowl, since the pursuit of these could be conducted throughout the year, in contrast to large game hunting, which was restricted in order to protect the species. Rare, sizeable or impressive birds such as pheasants, hazel grouse, herons, cranes, swans and peacocks were particularly valued. In late medieval Italy the wealthy raised peafowl on a moderate scale; still, the meat from these birds, although dry and tough, was among the most expensive available. In England, too, peafowl enjoyed a certain ranking at the dinner table from the thirteenth century onwards, although swan meat was more often served on special occasions. All in all, at the time, a number of bird species were eaten that

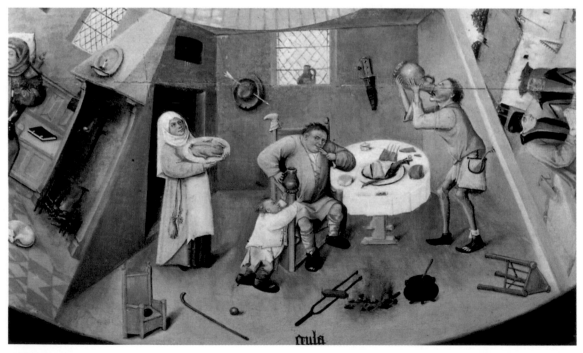

38 Different types of meat served at a burgher's house. Hams, trotters and sausages were associated with pigs and employed, as here, as symbols for gluttony. Gluttony appeared to be a progressive sin to medieval people, because it involved the degeneration of the natural desire for food and eventually led to moral corruption.

today's diner would be reluctant to have on his plate. Small birds, too, were part of the diet of the upper classes, and the cookery books of the era mention thrushes, warblers and woodcock. No doubt these were eaten at the tables of the poor as well, since it was harder then to monitor hunting than today. Rotisserie-roasted crane was a mouthwatering indulgence among the friars of German monasteries, as were quail of the smaller species, particularly in the spring-time. Songbirds were diligently caught with nets, and the fact that many monasteries were situated along the birds' migration routes facili-tated trapping them.

Of Brawn and Sausages

Many types of meat were also available out of season throughout the year, particularly meats that were salted. Parboiling or soaking the meat in water removed excess salt. According to an old Italian saying, meat should be eaten young and fish old or full-grown, and medical science endorsed this opinion. The meat of young animals was valued not only for its tenderness, but also for health reasons. Kid, veal and baby lamb were recommended. One- to two-year-old pigs were best, and wild boar was preferable to home-grown pork. According to the learned, animals dried up with age. Wild animals took more exercise and sun, and were in general warmer and drier than their domesticated counterparts.

Bird meat was considered healthier than red meat, and it was suggested especially for children and the weak and infirm. Of domestic fowl, hens and chickens were the most recommended,

having moderately warm and moist distinctive properties. Capons were at their best when young; if eaten old, they needed to be plump, since the caponizing process slowed down their natural drying process. Game birds had warm distinctive properties, although were a little too dry. On the list of favourites, following forest birds and pheasants, were waterfowl such as ducks. Chicken meat in particular was consumed in abundance in the Middle Ages.

In medieval cookery the entire animal was made thorough use of: head, brain, tongue, comb, neck, lungs, offal, belly and tripe, liver, kidneys, swim bladder, testicles, udder, teats, legs, tail and more. In addition to the actual meat cuts, offal was considered perfectly accept-able, even in the dishes of the upper classes. Brawns and jellies could be made from the heads and feet of animals, and, elaborately decorated and coloured, were handsome festive foods. For preservation as well as taste purposes, strong wines or a combination of vinegar and water were used as the cooking liquid for jellies. Swim bladders and animal cartilage and tendons served as coagulating agents. Congealing helped to preserve the ingredients and was, according to medical experts, pertinent to foodstuffs with particularly hot distinctive properties. As sustenance, jellies were best suited to those of hot and moist temperament, to the young and to the inhabitants of southerly regions during the dry times of the year.

Sauces were made from offal as well, usually gently simmered and seasoned with saffron and other spices. Occasionally cheese was added. Offal sauce is still a great delicacy today in, for instance, Normandy. Of the internal organs, lungs, hearts

39 Birds in a miniature by Évrard d'Espinques, 1480. Of all edible birds, songbirds and species with beautiful plumage were the most cherished, despite not being considered as flavoursome as chicken and other everyday poultry. One of the most popular dishes and a key item on festive occasions was white pudding, whose basic ingredients were bird meat and almonds. Rice, rice flour and milk could also be added. Prerequisites for the dish were a pale colour and a sweet flavour. The pudding was chilled and decorated with almonds or pomegranate seeds.

40 A farmer has slaughtered a pig and his wife is collecting the blood into a bowl, in this November calendar picture from the 1480s. The popularity of blood as an ingredient in food waxed and waned. In England it was possible to use blood as a cooking liquid; in Italy, for instance, this was not commonly done. In Finland the patties, nuggets, puddings and small pancakes made from blood, flour and fat are ancient heritage dishes. Fresh blood had been used since time immemorial in the hunter civilizations of the North. In the 1520s, at the dinner table of Hans Brask, Bishop of Linköping in Sweden, blood sausage was by no means sneered at. At these same dinners, many varieties of meat were consumed: meat pasties, pot roasts, smoked ox ribs, blood sausages, stuffed geese, chicken jelly with four stews, hazel grouse and wood-pigeons in butter sauce. For dessert, grapes, raisins and almonds were offered, while cakes and egg cheese rounded off the meal.

and stomachs were held in lesser esteem, and consequently mostly used for pie filling and sausages. Liver, on the other hand, was extremely highly rated, particularly birds' livers, which lent themselves well to sauces and as a colourant in other dishes. Brains, according to medical scientists, were hard to digest and spoiled easily; on the other hand, if prepared correctly, they constituted nutritious food that promoted the growth of the diner's own brain. Particularly recommended were the brains of small mountain birds, a delicacy rarely eaten these days.

Sausages may seem a modern concept, but the art of sausage-making has actually been around for a long time. In the Middle Ages sausages were among the most popular food

Animal Light

The fat, or tallow, derived from cows and sheep was an important component in candle-making at a time when electric light was unheard of. When animals were slaughtered in the autumn, tallow was set aside for candle-making. The fat was cut into pieces and melted over a low fire. Thick strands of yarn were suspended from a long stick and dipped into a tall receptacle containing the molten tallow. The partially formed candles were alternately cooled and dipped into the tallow until the desired thickness had been obtained.

The first references to candles date from 5,000 years ago. The Egyptians and Cretans dipped reed torches into molten cow and sheep tallow. In the Bible a candle is mentioned for the first time in conjunction with events dating back to around 900 BC.

Only the Romans began to systematically manufacture wax candles with a burnable centre. They did this by cleaning beeswax in seawater and pouring it, softened in the warmth of the sun, around a papyrus core coated with sulphur. The Romans used candles to conduct formal ceremonies and to illuminate their rooms. Today the oldest preserved candle is from second-century Avignon in France.

Before long the beeswax candle achieved an important place within the circles of the Catholic Church, and people began to celebrate Candlemas annually on the second day of February. In the twelfth century the tallow candle appeared commonly alongside the beeswax candle, being the principal source of light in well-to-do private homes throughout the Middle Ages. In the

fifteenth century beeswax candles were still exclusively burned in the churches, since the religious beliefs of the era drew a parallel between bees and paradise.

In church candles burned away sins and expelled evil forces, and were therefore required for many fundamental ecclesiastic procedures. During the darkest months of the year predictions for the future were read in the tallowy drips from candles. It was thought that on Christmas Eve, by candlelight, conversation with evil spirits could be conducted safely.

A candlestick-makers' guild was established in Paris in the mid-thirteenth century. The craftsmen travelled from house to house making candles from tallow that goodwives had set aside for them. A hundred years later, moulds were taken into use. However, the method of making beeswax candles by dipping yarn into molten beeswax was still being practised up until the twentieth century, when production-facilitating silicone was invented. In the nineteenth century the French chemist Michel-Eugène Chevreul discovered how to separate stearic acid from animal and vegetable fats. As a result, odour- and colourless stearin in candles soon became a substitute for animal tallow, which easily turned rancid. Cotton yarn had already replaced paper and string candlewicks.

products derived from meat, particularly at the tables of the poor. Converted into sausage, the shelf life of meat improved, and as merchandise sausages were hugely important. Although sausages could be bought ready-made, they were also prepared in private kitchens. Moreover they were deemed fit for the feasts of fashionable society, served either alone or as a base for another, more highly regarded meat variety, in order to create an impression of abundance. The Italian upper class favoured meat sausages made from pork, veal or liver. The filling was usually pressed into an animal intestine, stomach or other internal organ and formed into a cylindrical tube. Besides meat, it contained fat, cheese, herbs and spices, and the finished sausages could be boiled, smoked or grilled on a spit. In England boiling sausages was the most common cooking method, and plain water, an otherwise unusual cooking liquid, was often used for the process. An elegant dish for the tables of the upper classes could be created by dyeing sausage slices different colours.

From Simple Stews to Regal Roasts

The appreciation of meat manifested itself in the content of medieval cookery books: often as many as one-third of the recipes were for roasts, meat soups or stews. Most savoury bakery products contained meat, and it was also added to many vegetable dishes. Recipes including bird meat, particularly chicken, featured more than any others. In general people were advised to cook all meat thoroughly.

Peasants usually boiled their meat. Slow simmering would soften even a tough piece,

and meat of middling quality was better boiled than baked or roasted. In general boiled meat dishes were deemed inferior to those that were roasted, and better suited to everyday eating than to feasts.

Whole roasts were expensive and belonged to feasts, while lesser meat was generally chopped, minced or ground for cooking in stews, sauces, rissoles and pies. As previously mentioned, grilling, baking and rotisserie roasting on an open fire were cooking methods practised in

41 Seals of the Bruges butchers' guild from 1356. The corporation of master butchers was one of the most powerful associations in medieval cities, endowing its members with wealth and social leverage. In Paris alone, for instance, 250,000 animals are known to have been slaughtered in 1336. Laws regulated the work of professional butchers, who, at day's end, had to dispose of any unsold meat. To avoid the risk of spoilage, the butchered animals were bled forthwith.

the kitchens of the upper classes and urban residences rather than in rural areas and the homes of the common people. However, from a purely technical point of view, rotisserie roasting was a very simple procedure.

Often the roast constituted the main course at an upper-class event. Rotisserie roasting lent itself well to seasons in which an open fire was the principal source of heat, or to kitchens that were not equipped with ovens. In order to retain its succulence, the meat had to be protected from drying, and was therefore often coated with fat prior to being cooked. Frequently it was also basted with melted grease or other liquids during the cooking process. After roasting the meat might be glazed or stuffed to further bolster its moisture retention. It might also have been parboiled before being greased and roasted, in

order to render it as tender as possible. Being in charge of the roasting was in itself a venerable task, and the titles of royal rotisserie turner and meat carver were highly respected. The handling of roasts was part of the education of upper-class youths, and at royal courts the role of meat carver was assigned to knights.

Already in the Middle Ages, certain types of meat were associated with certain times of the year: pork and goose belonged to the meals of Advent and Christmas, and lamb to Easter. Mesmerized by meat as people in the Middle Ages were, they tended to combine different types of it in one and the same dish, possibly even more routinely and uninhibitedly than today. At a banquet, for instance, in order to make the utmost impression, bird meat could be stuffed with beef and the lot served with bacon. Sausages

42 Cooked meat is carved and arranged onto serving platters in this 14th-century illustration. The carving of meat into portions was a masculine task, and a nobleman would be well advised to learn the art in his youth. The side of an animal was sectioned one way; the rump, neck, breast and head another. Pheasants, partridges and ducks were all divided differently. As regards eating the meat, etiquette guides pointed out that dogs could be excused for gnawing the bones with their teeth, but a well-mannered diner would use his knife. The meat ought to be cut into small pieces on a plate and subsequently chewed for a while together with some bread before being swallowed. These guidelines were issued in the interest of good manners as well as good health.

could also be placed underneath a cut of meat, and a bird could be stuffed with pork. An entire line-up of meats was quite acceptable during one single meal: the bill of fare at a 1393 banquet in Paris for the gentry and the urban bourgeoisie included bone marrow pies, roasts with boiled pieces of meat, roast joints of game, chicken pasties, chicken-infused rice pudding in honey-sweetened almond milk, cuts of venison and other tasty treats.

Meat and the Feast

As already noted, meat-eating was particularly associated with festive occasions and indulgence in the Middle Ages. Eating meat was the antidote to the abstinence endured on fast days, and the contrast between ordinary and celebratory days became apparent in both the quantity and the quality of the food consumed.

The imagination of modern man has been captivated by the details that remain of the sumptuous royal feasts of the era. At the 1403 London wedding banquet for Henry IV of England and Joan of Navarre, the menu included some extraordinary meat courses:

1. Pieces of meat in galentine sauce, meat and rice, young swan, capons, pheasant
2. Venison in an acidic sauce, meat in aspic, pork, young rabbit, bittern, hazel grouse, boiled meat
3. Roast venison, woodcock, dotterel, rabbit, quail

At the June 1368 wedding banquet in Milan for Violante, daughter of Galeazzo II Visconti, and Duke Lionel of Clarence, the menu included a most respectable number of flamboyantly decorated and presented meat dishes.

FIRST COURSE: Gilded, fire-breathing pork, and gilded sea snail
SECOND COURSE: Gilded, golden-eyed rabbit, and gilded pike
THIRD COURSE: Gilded veal and gilded trout
FOURTH COURSE: Gilded quail and hazel grouse, and gilded roast trout
FIFTH COURSE: Gilded duck and heron, and gilded carp
SIXTH COURSE: Ox and capon in vinegar and garlic sauce, and sturgeon in broth
SEVENTH COURSE: Capon and meat in limonia sauce, and tench in limonia sauce
EIGHTH COURSE: Beef pies with cheese and eel pies
NINTH COURSE: Meat in aspic and fish in aspic
TENTH COURSE: Meat pudding and river lamprey pudding
ELEVENTH COURSE: Roast kid and roast sea needle
TWELFTH COURSE: Hare and kid in civere sauce and assorted fish in silvered civere sauce
THIRTEENTH COURSE: Venison and beef casserole, and pieces of fish
FOURTEENTH COURSE: Capon and chicken in a red and green sauce with oranges, and pieces of tench
FIFTEENTH COURSE: Peafowl and cabbage with beans and hashed tongue, and carp
SIXTEENTH COURSE: Roast rabbit, peafowl and duckling, and roast eel
SEVENTEENTH COURSE: Whey and cheese, and fruit and cherries

43 Copious amounts of meat were consumed at the banquets of the ruling classes. Peafowl, capon and partridge were signs of grandeur.

MEAT DISHES IN THE NORDIC COUNTRIES

In the Nordic countries the stores of meat for the winter season were accumulated during the summer and early autumn. Fresh meat was available mainly in the autumn during the slaughtering season, when most of it was salted and smoked for later use. Game was generally dried in the same way as fish. The peasants celebrated special occasions with game, porridge and bean dishes boosted with meat, while the well-to-do feasted on whole rotisserie-roasted roasts and chunks of meat simmered in various broths.

Entries of salted, smoked, dried and fresh meat appear in the sixteenth-century account books from Häme and Turku Castles, listing ox and beef, veal, mutton and lamb, pork, pork ribs, ham, bacon and suckling pig among the different types of meat. Offal and other internal organs were evidently much appreciated in the Nordic countries, too, as the ledgers go on to mention beef tongue, ox tongue, lamb and beef heart, liver, lungs and tripe. Sausages such as liverwurst and blood or meat sausages were also eaten, the Germans having passed on the art of sausage-making to the inhabitants of western Finland. The earliest particulars on Finnish sausages date from the 1540s, from Häme Castle and Kokemäki Manor. Among game, the castle account books mention venison, hare and wild-fowl, and among domestic fowl, geese and hens.

According to the 1546 ledgers, goose breasts, thighs and legs were among the delicacies served alongside beef tongues at the Turku Castle Bailiff's table. Meat dishes for the staff were made with beef, mutton, billy goat and ram. In 1563 the table of Duke John featured ham, bacon, beef back and tongue, offal, hare, wild fowl, venison and, on one occasion only, roe deer. The island of Ruissalo southwest of the city of Turku was the designated pleasure and hunting ground of the royal court, where red deer and other game had been introduced expressly for the Duke's hunting pleasure. Apart from that, venison was not very commonly consumed in medieval Turku, since the deer population had been hunted to extinction.

According to the directives in Mikael Agricola's *Rucouskiria Bibliasta*, the peoples of the North ought not, for health reasons, to partake of every type of meat in every season: as an illustration, goose and wild duck were to be avoided in February, and in June and July the same applied to suet and salted and fried meat.

44 The sea, the kingdom of the fishes, presented itself as both enchanting and dangerous to medieval man. Ahti (or Ahto) was the Finnish god of the sea and water, to whom the Finns of yore turned for success on their fishing and seal-hunting expeditions. In the legends of the *Kalevala*, the ancient Finnish folklore, Ahti was a regent and hero figure, although on many occasions also another designation for the god Lemminkäinen, whose character was a composite of several separate heroes. Ahti resided in Ahtola, the underwater kingdom. His wife was called Vellamo, and his daughters Annikki and Ahitar. The mythological underwater monsters were called Vetehinen and Iku-Turso.

five

BOUNTIES FROM THE DEEP

Fish consumption increased in the Middle Ages, as Christianity spread and the Catholic Church tightened its control. Fish played an important role in a food culture regulated by the mandatory observance of periods of fasting. In medieval thinking fish was associated with repentance: this cold and wet creature from the deep protected human flesh from excesses.

The intention of the Church was that lay Christians should practise fasting as an essentially voluntary, personal exercise in repentance. Religious orders and communities were a different matter. Naturally the Pope had to act as an example to others, and so, in the twelfth and thirteenth centuries, the edicts on ceremony communicated by the Curia included directives on the papal diet throughout the liturgical year. On Good Friday neither wine nor cooked food were to be served at the Pope's table – only water, bread and vegetables. In the Middle Ages members of the holy orders were perceived as fish eaters; however, eating habits among the religious elite and the worldly upper classes were often rather similar, and the majority of the senior clergy did not refuse meat outside the official periods of fasting.

Account books preserved from the Avignon papacy (1303–78) indicate that, in addition to fine meats, regular and generous supplies of fish were acquired for the papal kitchen from nearby rivers and lakes as well as the Mediterranean Sea and even the Atlantic Ocean. In 1320 the Pope's nephew was dispatched to La Rochelle on a mission to bring back cod and herring. Pope John XXII (1316–1334) repeatedly requisitioned eel and Mediterranean tuna, indulgences that later popes did not overly care for. The papal fish deliveries were also of interest to robbers: in 1383, 70 barrels of anchovies were made off with from one shipment.

Fish of Two Waters

Consumption of fish in the Middle Ages was so great that occasionally there was even a shortage of the commodity. Although fishing waters were to some extent subject to regulations similar to those of hunting grounds, the restrictions on the former were in general more lenient, and different social classes had greater liberty to fish than they had to hunt. The fish-rich rivers of Europe were divided into fishing districts. Freshwater fish caught in rivers were held in

Pisces salati

47 A fishmonger in a late 14th-century manuscript illustration. Getting hold of fresh fish was often an uncertain and problematic task in medieval cities. In medieval market towns specialist fish-mongers sold both freshwater and saltwater fish. Fresh fish was expensive and could be hard to come by, particularly in times of unrest. When, in the autumn of 1417, the civil war in France tore the nation apart, fish and other commodities were scarce in many regions, including the beleaguered Paris. The anonymous writer of the *Journal d'un bourgeois de Paris* bemoaned the price rises in the capital: a pound of salted butter now fetched up to two sous, while two or three eggs cost four sous and a small basket of fermented Baltic herring six deniers (one sou equalled twelve deniers). Fresh Baltic herring went for three to four blancs apiece, and inferior salted Baltic herring for two blancs (one blanc was roughly five deniers). Even the price of wine had escalated from two deniers a measure in August to four to six deniers in September.

were spawning: the piscine quarry was driven to a calm part of the river and virtually plucked out of the water. Smelt, whitefish and perch were particularly well suited to net bagging.

Salmon, mackerel and cod were trawled in the cold seas of the North. Boats from England fished waters as distant as the coast of Iceland, particularly after the Hanseatic League closed off all access to the Norwegian fishing banks. Herring was trawled off the coasts of Norfolk and

southern Lincolnshire – these waters gained further significance after the Baltic Sea suffered a steep decline in herring populations in the 1470s. In northern waters whales, harbour porpoises and seals were also hunted. These were considered fish – a convenient interpretation in regard to the prevailing rules on fasting. Towards the end of the Middle Ages the upper classes began to scoff at whale and cod being served at their tables, while harbour porpoise retained its reputation as a speciality food for periods of fasting. It was equally well suited to other grand occasions, such as the 1403 London wedding banquet for Henry IV of England and Joan of Navarre, where a variety of freshwater and saltwater fish featured prominently on the menu:

FIRST COURSE: Salted fish, strongly seasoned river lamprey, pike, bream and baked salmon

SECOND COURSE: Harbour porpoise, fish in aspic, bream, salmon, sea eel, sculpin, plaice and river lamprey pies

THIRD COURSE: Tench, trout, fried flounder, perch, baked river lamprey, loach, sturgeon and crabs

Up north in Finland, salted Baltic herring was an important export product. Cod, on the other hand, was dried for shipment overseas, while pike was exported live as well as dried. As much as half or more of all cod and Baltic herring consumed in Stockholm in the mid-sixteenth century came from the waters off the southwestern coast of Finland. Salted and dried fish not only served as everyday fare, but was also an important means of paying taxes to the Swedish Crown.

Pots, Pans and Gridirons: The Preparation of Fish

In the Middle Ages fish was preserved in a variety of ways – fermenting, drying, smoking and salting – in order to be available throughout the year. Owing to the rules on fasting, recipes for fish dishes made up a considerable portion of medieval cookery books; in certain fifteenth-century volumes up to a quarter of the collected cooking instructions were for fish dishes, despite fish being perceived as less of an upper-class food product than meat.

Fish could be poached, fried in a cast iron or copper pan, grilled on a gridiron or baked inside a pie or a pastry shell – in short, it could be cooked in a number of ways. Grilling inside a hinged gridiron lent itself well to small fish in particular, since those could be cooked whole without cleaning. When pan-frying fish, oil was used as the cooking grease, and normally the flesh was not breaded or dusted with flour. As fish had moist and cold distinctive properties, medical experts were keen to suggest pan-frying or grilling it, and serving it with a sauce rich in spices and herbs with warm and dry properties. If the fish ended up being poached, it was to be done very thoroughly, due to its moist distinctive

48 Pike fishing in the North in a 16th-century woodcut. In Finland, at the royal castles of Turku and Häme, the kitchens used not only salted and dried fish, but also smoked and fresh. Mentioned in the 16th-century ledgers are perch, eels, pike, flounders, smelt, bream, salmon and salmon roe, dried rays, whitefish and whitefish roe, Baltic and North Atlantic herrings, roach, ide, cod and vimba bream, as well as assorted salted fish and fish dried on skewers over an open flame. At the Turku Castle bailiff's table in 1546, salmon, salted perch and a selection of other salted fish were served, in addition to Norwegian stockfish and dried bream, ide and herring. Over at the servants' table, the staff had salted salmon and whitefish and various roes. In 1563 the table of Duke John held salmon, cod, Baltic herring, smoked whitefish and Skåne herring from the southernmost county of Sweden, among other treats.

properties. To avoid the flesh breaking into pieces, the poaching was done over a low flame, usually in just a small amount of water, sometimes combined with vinegar or wine. In England, fish was sometimes poached in beer.

The internal organs of fish were also made thorough use of, for instance in soups and sauces. In addition to swim bladders, assorted fish roes were employed in the congealing process of pastries and fish dishes, while sturgeon roe was used for caviar and eaten as a delicacy with, for instance, a piece of toasted bread, just like today. Fish could be prepared in the same way as meat when making savoury aspics and different types of sausages for the tables of the rich during a period of fasting. In the white pudding made especially for fasts, fish replaced fowl; in English recipes perch, haddock or lobster were the recommended main ingredients. During a period of fasting the meal was often finished off with nuts, whose distinctive

properties were the opposite of those of fish. However, warm apples and pears taken together with sweet confectionery could also constitute the final course. The fish recipes in this book include several ingredients and seasonings that counter the 'dangerous' properties of fish.

Oysters and mussels were also used in food preparation. Oysters were popular among the rich, although the poor, too, were occasionally able to afford them. Mussels and other molluscs were seasoned and cooked in their own broth or in a concoction of, say, eggs, wine, almonds, pieces of bread and assorted exotic spices. Crayfish, shrimp and lobsters could also be oven-baked. In England most fish dishes were served cold; in Italy fish, crustaceans and mussels were generally served warm, leaving only jellies and aspics to be served cold.

According to medieval medical opinion, fish was not a particularly nutritious or praiseworthy food. Yet because of the requirements laid down

49 A crab by Albrecht Dürer.

82

by the Church with regard to fasting, the views of medical experts had little bearing on people's diets. Saltwater fish were in general deemed more beneficial to human health than their freshwater counterparts, since the salinity of the sea was thought to have a drying effect on this inherently moist creature.

The fish dishes on the menus and in the recipe collections that remain with us today speak of the gastronomic values and traditions of the medieval upper classes in particular. To the twenty-first-century reader some of the preparations sound delicious; others come across as quite extraordinary. Guests at a 1393 banquet in Paris given for members of the gentry and the urban bourgeoisie were treated to cod liver and bone marrow pasties, eel in a purée of spices, cold fish in sage sauce, bream with eel pasties,

river lamprey in pepper sauce, fried bream with cream pies and sturgeon, as well as other assorted saltwater and freshwater fish. At a German banquet in the early modern period diners feasted on stockfish with oil and raisins, bream fried in oil, boiled eel with pepper, grilled Baltic herring with mustard, fish in an acidic sauce, carp, pike and trout simmered in ginger broth.

With the help of different kinds of fish, the social position of diners could be demonstrated according to the same principles as when serving meat. At the household of Henry Percy, Earl of Northumberland (1341–1408), the host couple enjoyed oven-baked herring or sprat dishes for breakfast on days of fasting, while close relatives were given sprat and salted fish, and the lowest-ranking members of the household salted fish only.

50 In Dirk Bouts's painting Mary Magdalene washes the feet of Christ with her tears and hair as a token of humility and repentance. The friar kneeling by the door on the right has commissioned the painting. The fish laid out on the table allude to Jesus and the Last Supper. Ichthys is the ancient Greek word for fish, but the letters spelling it also appear in the litany *Iesous Christos Theou Hyios Sootēr*, or Jesus Christ, Son of God, the Saviour. Thus early Christians adopted the fish as the secret sign of Christ – the ideogram symbolizing the idea of Christianity. The motif appears in several early Christian monuments and catacombs. Fish frequently surfaced in the Bible, too, where the scriptures told of Peter catching fish (Luke 5:1–11) and other fish-related miracles (John 6:1–13, Tobias 6:1–9). Jesus and his apostles were the fishers of men's souls. In the theological symbolism of the Middle Ages the fish became the metaphor of Christian abstinence and repentance. Since it also served as sustenance, of which the resurrected Christ himself had partaken, it became the symbol of the Last Supper in the visual arts of Christianity. The fish resided in the sea; therefore it also referred to the religious rite of baptism.

According to the early Christian author Tertullian (c. 155–222), the newly christened human born out of the baptismal water was like a small fish, the image of Christ himself. In medieval art the fish was also the distinctive mark of a multitude of saints, among them St Brendan (c. 489– c. 583), protector of seafarers, and St Anthony of Padua (1195–1231), who was said to have spread the gospel among fish.

Fermenting and drying were the traditional and widely used methods for preserving fish in the Far North. In Finland an expression tentatively interpreted as 'lying fallow' was used with reference to fish put up for fermenting. The country's historical sources mention fermented fish less frequently than dried fish, for the reason that the former were rarely used for tax-paying purposes, but merely for home consumption.

Drying was a more widespread and practical preservation method than fermenting, since it facilitated the transportation and storage of fish. In Finland dried fish was generally referred to as *kapakala*, or stockfish, and the drying process was colloquially called *kapaaminen*. The old Nordic words *thorsk*, *torsk* and *turska*, all meaning 'cod', bear testimony to the central role of drying fish in Scandinavia, tracing back to the Indo-Germanic verb *ters*, ' to dry'. In sixteenth-century Scandinavian documentation dried fish appears under several designations: *torrfisk*, *torra gäddor* (dried pike), *torr idh* (dried ide), *krampe sill* (herring reduced or contracted in size) and *spettfisk* (fish dried on a spit). In certain account books dried pike is often synonymous with Finnish pike, *finska gäddör*.

Usually the drying process took place out-doors in the wind and sun; oven drying became common only in the modern era. Both large and small fish were dried outdoors. Larger fish such as bream, pike and pike-perch were split and dried on sticks fastened to the outside walls of buildings. They could also be suspended from the slats or nailed directly into the walls. Smaller fish like perch, roach and Baltic herring were strung onto twine to dry. The very smallest species such as bleak, smelt and vendace were laid out on boards or in baskets to dry in the sun.

Dried fish could be eaten plain, perhaps on an outing as part of a packed meal, or it could be brought along on a visit as a present to the host. In winter it made a fine accompaniment to soups or stews, and in years of famine, ground, dried fish served as a supplement to flour in bread. More usually, however, dried fish was boiled before being eaten. The biggest fish — pike-perch, pike and burbot — were used for lutefisk.

Dried fish were stored in a number of ways: the bigger specimens were suspended from the rafters and the smaller placed in woven bushels, or the fish could be salted, even after being dried, a stone weighing them down in the salting vats. In other words, the drying and salting methods complemented each other. In the 1550s, at the royal estate of Rantasalmi in Finland, the custom was to dry the fish caught in the spring and to salt the fish caught in the autumn. In his 1555– 6 cata-logue of complaints about the misdemeanours of the aristocracy, Jakob Larsson Teit, secretary to Gustav Vasa of Sweden, mentions salted cod and Baltic herring, dried pike and Pernaja smelt as well as dried Baltic herring, perch and roach.

Salting was a more recent preservation method than drying, the earliest documentation on the subject dating from the end of the Middle Ages. Salt was expensive and required in great quantities — in salted Baltic herring, for instance, the salt content amounted to as much as one-third of the overall weight. In the sixteenth century the Swedish Crown aimed to switch from dried to salted fish; consequently in all Nordic royal castles and manor houses dried fish was treated with salt provided by the Crown. As

Charlemagne, although the practice had been known from antiquity. In more northern latitudes the art of smoking fish is likely to have spread by way of the northwestern corner of the German states. The oldest known Nordic sources to mention smoked fish are the Swedish Enköping Hospital codes of conduct of 1367–83. The Swedish ecclesiastic Olaus Magnus's description of smoking fish in the North is also known far and wide. The oldest Finnish information on the subject dates from 1544, from Kokemäki Estate in the southwestern part of the country.

Apparently, then, fish on the sixteenth-century Nordic royal estates was preserved using three different methods: drying, salting and smoking. Depending on the availability of salt and the time of the year the fish was caught, the catch was either salted or dried outdoors, with the exception of some of the nobler species such as salmon and whitefish, which were smoked indoors, producing what is called *spickelax* and *spickesik*. Initially, however, the majority of fish were dried outdoors, although that method was gradually discontinued as salt became more readily available. For a long time the new, fast-acting method of hot-smoking remained relatively rare and, if used, was applied mainly to the preparation of gourmet foods. And so it continued to be, as salt became a more commonly used commodity, and hot-smoking, for that matter, did not produce long-lasting fish.

a rule sea fish were set aside for salting, since freshwater fish were preferably purchased and consumed fresh in the interior of the country. In order to remove excess salt, salted fish had to be soaked thoroughly before being used, just like salted meat. Salted fish is rarely mentioned in medieval cookery books, since the wealthy did not overly care for it, wishing instead to see as much fresh fish as possible on their tables.

Drying could also be paired with smoking. Initially a slow drying-cum-smoking technique was used, from which a faster hot-smoking method developed at the end of the Middle Ages. In Central Europe, for instance, details on smoking fish exist from the ninth-century court of

52 Preparing verjus sauce from raw grapes. Since verjus is hard to come by in shops today, red wine vinegar, lemon juice or apple cider vinegar diluted with water can be used as a substitute (three parts vinegar or juice to one part water).

six

INGENIOUS SAUCES, SEDUCTIVE SPICES

Sauces played an important part in the food culture of the Middle Ages. Their function was to elevate the standard of various dishes to their own level, and to bring variety to foods of similar character. Many cookbooks included a separate chapter or passage on sauces, while a good chef was first and foremost an excellent sauce-maker. In the food culture of the upper classes practically every dish came with its own sauce. There were also free-standing sauces, which could be served with a variety of dishes according to preference. An upper-class household might also include a designated member of staff whose task it was to select and combine the appropriate sauce with every type of food prepared. In England this fell upon the carver, while in France the person was called *l'écuyer tranchant*. At banquets sauces could either be poured directly over meat or served in small dishes for dipping. In royal households there might also be a separate office of the kitchen consigned for sauce-making (the *sawsery*), a concept that emphasized the overall importance of sauce.

Sauces were widely used by the lower classes as well. They were made at home, although in

cities ready-made sauces were also on offer. In France professional sauce-makers, *les sauciers*, formed their own organization, giving them exclusive control over the making and selling of sauces.

Sauces were important when it came to flavouring a dish, although their function was also to stimulate the appetite and alleviate any harmful properties that other ingredients might have. Some medical experts were of the opinion that tasty sauces caused people to eat more than was good for them. The fourteenth-century Italian physician and astrologer Maino de' Maineri believed that a healthy human being should consume sauces in small quantities only, and that the more the temperament of a sauce differed from the other ingredients in a dish, the less of it ought to be consumed. Medical science was particularly rigorous in its opinions on sauces suitable for fish, something that cookery books, too, defined in greater detail than they did sauces for meat. Citrus juices, vinegar and mustard were appropriate condiments for fish, as were green, white and garlic-flavoured sauces.

There were also some extremely uncomplicated and easily prepared sauce alternatives to hand. In the South the juice from a citrus fruit,

53 Fruit trees in a medieval miniature. In the Middle Ages fruit juices often served as the base for various sauces.

for instance, could be pressed directly onto meat, poultry or fish in lieu of a sauce. Grape juice to which nothing but herbs had been added was used in a similar fashion. A wine reduction could also serve as a sauce. Sometimes even plain salt mixed with an acidic juice might act as a passable condiment. The Italian writer Bartolomeo Platina (1421–1481) was of the opinion that a sauce blended from oil, vinegar and salt sufficed for fresh lettuce and boiled vegetables. Vinegar could also be used as a sauce, either plain or seasoned with salt and ginger, although with a person's welfare in mind, it was more beneficial when sweetened with honey or sugar. Vinegar sauce was suggested especially for fish, since it neutralized the detrimental properties of the latter. Pure herbal juice could also function as a sauce; on festive occasions the *cokentrice*, or half capon, half pig, was often served with parsley juice. The dripping from a roast could be used not only as a basting agent, but as a sauce too.

Plain mustard also passed as an accompaniment to both fish and poultry. In the Middle Ages mustard was an everyday commodity that was used in extremely large quantities. It could be added to complicated sauces that were equally well suited to fish, meat or game such as wild boar. Mustard was made from crushed mustard seeds mixed with verjus, or the liquid pressed from raw wine grapes. Mustard combined with vinegar was a potent medicament that cleared the head and eased the spirit. It kept for a long time and therefore did not have to be prepared immediately before use, but could be stored. A similar condiment with a long shelf life was the Italian acidic orange compote (*savore aranzato*), which kept for up to a year.

As previously mentioned, a distinct particularity of medieval sauces was the general use of soft white bread as a binding agent, rather than wheat flour. Other common binders were ground almonds, eggs, bird livers and, occasionally, rice flour. A fashionably tart flavour was often attempted and achieved with the help of sharp-tasting liquids such as wine, vinegar, citrus fruit juices or verjus.

The word 'sauce' comes from the Latin *salsus*, or the past participle of *salere*, 'to salt'. The ancient Romans did indeed concoct some rather salty sauces, although in the medieval kitchen assorted spices and aromatic herbs replaced the salt. French cookery books such as the *Viandier* and the *Ménagier de Paris* list a fair amount of spices in their sauce recipes. Up to sixteen different spices and herbs could be included in a single sauce. In order to achieve as smooth a product as possible, the ingredients for a sauce were first thoroughly crushed in a mortar and then passed through a sieve at the finishing stage. Colour and taste were of the essence, often determining the name of the sauce. *Cameline* sauce got its name from its brown colour and the cinnamon it contained; *poivrande* sauce from pepper (*pevrada*, the peppery one).

Sauces were often grouped into two main categories: cooked and uncooked. The ingredients in an uncooked sauce usually consisted of white bread and ground almonds, with grape juice, vinegar or wine, and sometimes beef stock or milk as the liquid. A common and popular uncooked cold sauce was the aforementioned cinnamon-flavoured *cameline* sauce, which was well suited to either meat or fish. A widely recognized, basic cooked sauce was the ginger-flavoured *jance*. Both sauces also came in garlic-flavoured versions.

Sauces could also be grouped into fruit sauces and spice sauces. The ingredients in fruit sauces were plums, grapes, mulberries and cherries, which gave the sauce a sweetish flavour. Sugar was often added; salt, on the other hand, rarely so. Vast amounts of vinegar or similar liquids could also be fermented from fruit sauces. Common spice sauces were primarily garlic sauces, well suited to a large number of dishes. There, too, a tangy flavour was popular. Beef or fish stock together with almonds and white bread were used in the preparation of garlic sauces (*agliata* in Italian, *aillée* in French). Garlic sauce tinged with dark grapes went well with light-coloured bird dishes, for instance.

Pepper sauce was a common spice sauce served with venison, hare, wild boar or any other

54 A chef and an aide prepare brews, baked meats and sauces. The chef tastes the food.

strong-flavoured game. It was prepared by boiling toasted bread in blood or offal, and adding peppered vinegar to the mixture. Pepper sauces were suitable for fish as well.

Pepper sauce was immensely popular in England, while fruit and garlic sauces were Italian favourites. That said, *galentyne* sauce was the preferred sauce of the English upper classes, and went well with both fish and meat. It was made with bread soaked in vinegar, and seasoned with cinnamon, ginger and often also galangal rhizome, a spice related to the ginger root – hence, possibly, the name of this sauce. When served with eel and pike, *galentyne* sauce was flavoured with garlic.

The Noble Art of Seasoning

One particularity of the medieval kitchen was its wide variety of herbs and spices, and the diversity with which these were implemented and combined. In vegetable dishes and dishes with mild flavours, though, spices were used sparingly; in soups, for instance, spices and herbs were often not added until the final stage of the cooking process, so as not to lose their aroma.

The seasoning had to be pulverized, and was therefore crushed in a mortar prior to being added to a sauce or a dish. The main ingredients could also be rolled in spices, or spices could be rubbed onto the surface of, say, a piece of meat or fish. Spices were also sprinkled on top of dishes that had already been cooked as a finishing touch. Exotic spices from faraway places could be enjoyed at the end of a meal as well, either plain or coated with sugar. It is difficult to tell exactly how generously spices were being utilized, since exact quantities are not given in recipes. Adding seasoning was a noble art that required the skill of combining and harmonizing different flavours. Because most spices were expensive, they were probably used with consideration and only as needed. Chilli peppers, paprika and vanilla were unknown in the Middle Ages; otherwise more or less the same herbs and spices were used then as today. Spices were regarded as luxury items of a certain value, and were therefore usually stored in a locked spice cupboard. In England upper-class households kept their own spice office – the spicery – where other costly ingredients such as rice, speciality wines and dried fruits were also stored. In the Middle Ages the word 'spice' stood for all that was rare and expensive.

Since most spices were imported from afar and therefore expensive, they left a mark on the

55 Venetian merchants disembarking at the port of Cambaet in India in an illustration from *The Travels of Marco Polo*. The great medieval infatuation with exotic spices is well known. The Crusades (1095–1270) familiarized Europeans with novelty spices from the East. Ships carried food and clothing to the pilgrims, and brought back spices, exotic fruits and precious stones on their return. In 1271 Venetian-born Marco Polo (1254–1324), the great adventurer of the high seas, set out on a voyage around the world, to return some twenty years later to his home harbour, his ships laden with spices. His tales from his travels to faraway lands enthralled people of the late Middle Ages. Polo told about the natural riches of the natives he had met: black pepper, nutmeg, galangal, cloves and other spices. In the Europe of Marco Polo's time, economic growth and the conquest of Muslim territories increased people's desire to obtain unfamiliar and exotic products from the East. Spices captivated their imagination, and made them dream of distant lands as they smelled and tasted the aromatic substances. Spices symbolized the world yet to be conquered, spelling adventure and escape – and peril.

financial world, too: the word 'spice' (*épice* in French) came from the Latin *species*, meaning 'money'. In the Middle Ages the custom was to settle legal expenses, taxes and debts with pepper and other spices, pepper often also forming part of a dowry. After a case in court it was customary for the winning party to offer their legal representative a selection of delectable spices, the so-called *épices des juges*. This could consist of ginger confectionery, cardamom squares, nutmeg jam and sugar.

Through the use of spices it was possible to distinguish oneself from others and proclaim one's social standing. Spicy dishes and drinks were not merely a question of the personal taste preferences of the elite. The purchase and use of spices reflected class differences in society. The upper classes bought saffron, ginger, cloves, nutmeg, cinnamon and other faraway spices at great expense. The wealthy bourgeoisie strived to attain a social level equal to that of the aristocracy, and so spent vast amounts on spices.

The poor bought ready-made, inexpensive blends, and the very poorest made do with onion and garlic.

Spices were especially important on special occasions, when their role was to communicate the wealth and social standing of the organizer of the event. However, spices and herbs were also used for health reasons in both everyday and celebratory cooking. Furthermore, as already noted, it was not the purpose of spices to conceal the flavour of spoilt food. Those who could afford to buy expensive spices were also able to obtain high-quality ingredients.

Spices from Faraway Lands: Flavours from the Ends of the Earth

The classification of spices, aromatic herbs and plants used as seasoning was somewhat vague in the Middle Ages. The category of spices could also include lemons, dates and the leaves of orange trees. According to one method of categorizing, the principal spices, or gross spices, included ginger, cinnamon, grains of paradise (also known as melegueta pepper) and pepper, while among the lesser, or minor, spices were nutmeg, cloves, mace and galangal.

In the Middle Ages pepper was the most significant imported spice – the 'king of spices'. Large amounts of pepper had been used in the ancient Roman kitchen. However, from the fourteenth century onwards, the use of pepper diminished to some extent as the more economical grains of paradise, the peppery seeds of a West African plant of the ginger family, rose in popularity. The increasing popularity of aromatic herbs also unsettled the good standing of pepper,

although pharmacists continued to use the spice regularly as a medicine for headaches, anaemia and lack of appetite, and as an antidote for poison. Pepper was good for coughs, liver and stomach ailments, abscesses, chest pains, fevers and shivering fits, night blindness, excess body moisture and embittered hearts. Black, white, long and round pepper were all on offer. The poor used juniper berries as a substitute, which tasted of resin and went well with strongly flavoured game. The berries were also recommended for gluttons, since they stimulated the gastric fluids.

The fierily pungent ginger was greatly valued in the Middle Ages and before. In ancient Greece it was used in a number of dishes and drinks, being a propitious ingredient in elixirs of love. Furthermore it was a potent remedy for colds, and an effective prophylactic against pestilence and scurvy. The ginger plant was thought to originate in the Near East, although the Arabs had in fact brought it with them from India. Today, too, ginger is an important spice in Middle and Far Eastern cooking. In the Middle Ages the ginger root was forgiven its unsightly outer appearance for the sake of its fine fragrance. It was used to flavour a number of drinks, and eaten both fresh and preserved in jams and marmalades. Ginger was often stored in honey to prevent its aroma from fading.

According to medieval medical experts, ginger was thirst-quenching as well as invigorating for the brain. It improved the appetite and set the digestive juices flowing, and many a festive meal was therefore finished with ginger confectionery. Ginger had long been known as a therapeutic plant, and in recent years researchers have noted that it is an exceptionally potent remedy for coughs. In addition it alleviates aches and pains, lowers the body temperature, stimulates the immune system and calms and strengthens the heart. Moreover it acts as an antioxidant and may kill salmonella bacteria. It can also serve as a meat-softening agent and prolong the shelf life of meat, and it can prevent seasickness and lower cholesterol. As a result, people in the past fared very well from their affection for ginger.

The galangal rhizome resembles its relative, the ginger root. Galangal is indigenous to China, and the Tatars are said to have used it as flavouring in their tea. In the late Middle Ages galangal was known in places as remote as the Nordic countries: in Mikael Agricola's book of prayers (*Rucouskiria*, 1544), readers were encouraged to take strong, warming spices such as ginger, pepper, galangal and cloves during the cold days of January. They were recommended to mix some spirits with the spices, but not to add honey to the drink, and 'not to bleed the main arteries, but only the hepatic vein, and only if the need arises'.

Galangal can be obtained from both the greater galangal (*Alpinia galanga*) and the lesser galangal (*Alpinia officinarum*) plants. The greater galangal is a plant of the Thai, Indonesian and Malay subcontinent and requires tropical conditions, whereas the lesser galangal, reddish of colour and stronger of taste, also grows in slightly more temperate climates. The flavour of fresh galangal rhizome is similar to that of ginger, although with resinous, camphoric undertones.

Cinnamon, too, was valued in the Middle Ages. Even in ancient times the Egyptians had used cinnamon in their embalming rituals. In Rome Emperor Nero (AD 37–68) ordered his entire annual supply of cinnamon set on fire as a sign of remorse after having killed his wife in a fit of temper. In the Old Testament cinnamon was mentioned as being more precious than gold. The late twelfth-century French poet Chrétien de Troyes sang its praises in his *Perceval, le Conte du Graal* (*Perceval, the Story of the Grail*), since cinnamon was said to have scented the blood of Christ in the Holy Grail. In the medieval kitchen the spice was used in both savoury and sweet dishes. Cinnamon sticks were added to jams and hot wine, while ground cinnamon flavoured biscuits, cakes and pies. Doctors prescribed cinnamon for trapped wind and other gastric discomforts suffered after excess feasting.

In the Middle Ages saffron was the most expensive spice of all, costing twelve times the price of ginger. In France a *livre* (approx. 490 g) of saffron sold for the same price as a horse, a *livre* of ginger for the price of a sheep, and two *livres* of mace for the price of a cow. In upper-class kitchens saffron was the most widely used spice in a number of dishes and sauces, and owing to its intense flavour only a tiny amount was needed to season one portion of food. Saffron was not only used as a flavouring, but also as a food colouring or dye. The author of the *Mesnagier de Paris* suggested substituting saffron with egg yolks, if so desired; these were less expensive but still provided a golden-yellow colour.

In the late Middle Ages saffron was no longer uniquely from faraway lands, but was cultivated closer at hand as well – in Italy, for instance. All the same, it was still expensive. Saffron is

PROFUSION OF FLAVOURS

Researchers have noted that the Europeans in the Middle Ages shared a fondness for a profusion of flavours, but that the preferences differed somewhat by region. The French availed themselves of spices with greater diversity than others, favouring ginger and cinnamon and combinations of the two, and also grains of paradise, which were used less commonly elsewhere. In the cookery books of medieval Italy pepper, cloves, ginger and cinnamon appear most frequently among the foreign spices imported from afar. The Italians also had a liking for aromatic herbs. In England the most common exotic spice after saffron was ginger, whereas grains of paradise were less usual. Cinnamon is mentioned more often in English cookery books than in those of Italy.

Written references often provide information on the use of spices that conflicts with archaeological evidence. Pepper, by way of illustration, is highlighted in German cookery books; yet in archaeological findings it does not stand out as clearly among other spices. According to archaeological research, exotic spices were more common in northern Germany and northern Poland than in Scandinavia and Estonia.

Account books preserved from the banquets of the Tallinn municipal authorities and professional guilds during the years from 1404 to 1554 inform us that ginger, pepper, saffron, mustard, cloves, cinnamon, anise, grains of paradise, caraway and nutmeg were predominantly used. In the Nordic countries ledgers indicate that great amounts of honey, vinegar, anise, caraway, cloves and black pepper were consumed at the tables of the elite. ◁

56 Herbs from a herb garden are selected for cooking in an illustration from a medieval manuscript.

derived from the dried stigmas of the saffron crocus (*Crocus sativus*), which belongs to the iris family. These perennial plants with corms are native to the warmer regions of Eurasia. One kilogram of saffron requires approximately half a million stigmas, hand-picked from the pistils of the crocus flowers, and one flower alone yields only three threads. Saffron is still the most expensive spice in the world, costing approximately €5,000 per kilogram.

Cardamom, obtainable from Indian rainforests, was the second most expensive spice in the Middle Ages. The King of Babylon raised cardamom in his own gardens in 721 BC, and it was highly appreciated in ancient Greece and Rome as well. After the Middle Ages cardamom lost its popularity. The flavour of cardamom is warm and citric, and a small amount of the spice sufficed for seasoning a dish. Cardamom lent itself well to both savoury and sweet foods, from meat dishes to apple pies. In the Middle Ages it was also added to various brews such as *claret*, a popular wine-based drink. Cardamom was also thought to relieve certain health problems, such as urinary complaints. In the Nordic countries cardamom became common only towards the end of the Middle Ages.

Cloves gave precious acerbity to food in the Middle Ages, and were unequalled as flavouring in a number of drinks. The clove is a tree of the myrtle family that grows in India and its neighbouring regions, and the dried flower buds are used as a spice. In classical times cloves had lent their flavour to a number of wines, and the Greeks and Romans also used the spice to perfume their bodies. In the Middle Ages cloves were recommended for the infirm: two buds

added to boiling, sugar-sweetened water sufficed if they were steeped for half an hour before the mixture was ingested.

Nutmeg was a costly spice that arrived in Europe with the Arabs from across the Indian Ocean. It was derived from the seeds and inflorescence of the nutmeg tree in the genus *Myristica*. Just as it is today, the nutmeg seed was used with caution in the Middle Ages due to its hallucinatory properties induced by a narcotic called myristin, a potentially poisonous substance if taken in large quantities. Mace was also used in the Middle Ages as flavouring in a number of dishes. In several of the recipes in this book a pinch of nutmeg or mace is suggested.

Aromatic Herbs

Those in the Middle Ages who could not afford expensive, exotic spices from faraway lands used aromatic herbs and plants to flavour their food. Herbs were added to dishes either fresh or dried, chopped or gently sautéed in fat. Special herb dishes were also to be had, many of which were particularly appropriate during periods of fasting.

Parsley, marjoram, fennel, hyssop, mint and basil were common kitchen herbs, while chervil, dill and rosemary were also popular. However, the use of herbs varied according to region. Oregano and basil are rarely mentioned in Italian cookery books, although they were grown in Italy. One theory is that they were produced more for pharmaceutical purposes than for food. Marjoram, caraway, coriander and anise were heard of, although the first three were hardly ever referred to in English cookery books, lct alone oregano or basil. Sage, hyssop and savory appeared in their stead, being domestic herbs that succeeded better in northerly climates. Parsley was also used with great diversity in England and other European countries, being both decorative and good-tasting. In the Nordic countries the use of parsley and coriander did not become wide-spread until much later in the Middle Ages.

Caraway was equally popular, being well suited to fish, for instance. Medical experts also believed caraway to be an efficient remedy for stomach troubles. According to one recipe for a curative potion, the caraway seeds were first crushed in a mortar and then boiled in beer. Any surface foam was skimmed off, and the liquid was passed through a piece of gauze, after which it was offered to the patient to be taken warm. The strained caraway seeds were wrapped in a linen cloth, and the warm compress placed onto the abdomen of the patient. A blend of anise, caraway, ginger, nutmeg and mint was also helpful in the

57 Medicinal herbs in their planters in a 16th-century woodcut. To some extent the theories of medical experts influenced the way people in the Middle Ages – the wealthy in particular – decided on spices and herbs for their dishes. The healthy strived to select seasoning that conformed to their specific temperament and state of health. For the ailing, the physicians recommended certain spices based on their curative properties. In France the city of Montpellier was famous for its trade in spices, and from the 11th century onwards knowledge of spices and their usage was also taught at the city's medical faculty, which was soon to be world-renowned.

treatment of stomach complaints and lack of appetite. Constitutionally caraway, anise and fennel were considered the warmest seeds and therefore the best at boosting the digestive capability of the stomach.

Sage, however, was the most significant of all aromatic herbs. It is frequently mentioned in French cookery books such as the *Viandier* and the *Ménagier de Paris*. Sage had a pleasant flavour that went well in a number of dishes and drinks. Physicians of antiquity and the Middle Ages greatly valued the therapeutic properties of the herb, whose name derives from the Latin word *salva*, 'to save'. In Finland the Naantali Abbey fifteenth-century book on herbs mentions sage, while Mikael Agricola's book of prayers urges people in the North to use sage, particularly in the months of June and July.

Practically all vegetables could also be used as seasoning. Although garlic, onions and shallots were often thought of as food for peasants, they, too, had a place at the tables of the aristocracy. Garlic in particular was a common and popular plant that worked excellently as seasoning, cooked vegetable and medicinal herb. Efforts to tackle the malodorous after-effects of garlic included eating breath-freshening herbs and drinking vinegar. Garlic sauce was particularly well liked when taken with various fish and meat dishes.

The health-promoting properties of garlic have long been known. The Greek physician Hippocrates (*c.* 460–*c.* 370 BC) had praised the beneficial qualities of the plant, attesting to its hot, laxative and diuretic qualities. The Crusaders used garlic to protect themselves from pestilence and demons, and doctors prescribed the plant

MEDICINAL HERBS

To counter mental stress, medical experts in the Middle Ages used herbs such as sage, balm, rosemary, St John's wort and valerian. Rhinitis and common colds were treated with lilac, elder, chamomile, mullein, lungwort, burnet, linden flower and thyme. Hops, valerian and lavender were good for sleeplessness, while milk thistle, seaside centaury, geum, peppermint and dandelions soothed stomach ills. For intestinal complaints, plantain, senna and flax were recommended, and lesions and wounds were treated with comfrey, calendula, tormentil, horsetail and arnica.

Agrimony, celery seeds, common rue, pennyroyal, common betony, wormwood, bittersweet nightshade, fennel, sage, black elder, celery root and nettles, among others, are herbs recommended in the health instructions in Mikael Agricola's book of prayers.

Several types of strong-scented rue were used to counter plague and other serious conditions, and to keep away vermin and snakes. In churches common rue, or herb-of-grace, was rubbed onto the floor to banish witches. Potions made from rue were thought to improve a person's health in general, and to dispel depression, calm the spirit, enhance reasoning and logical thought and restrain sexual desires, as well as countering rheumatism, gout, neurological disorders, heart and stomach complaints and external abrasions and afflictions of the skin. Cautiously apportioned, dried rue leaves were used as seasoning for meat and vegetable dishes and as a colouring for wine — in overly large quantities, rue became poisonous.

Betony was thought to treat jaundice, epilepsy and gout as well as headaches and toothaches. It was also used in witchcraft and for the eviction of evil forces, and burned in bonfires and incense. It was tucked inside pillows to prevent nightmares, and used as filling in fortune-bringing amulets.

Moths and other insects could be dispelled with the help of wormwood. The leaves and shoots of the plant were used to make powders, tinctures, salves and brews for the treatment of stomach ailments and the expulsion of parasitic worms in both humans and animals, and to relieve rheumatism and other aches and pains, including skin infections, coughs, ear, tooth and eye infections, bone diseases and disorders of the mind. Wormwood was also used in love potions and as a flavouring for beer, wine and spirits.

as a preventive against rheumatism. Garlic also dilated blocked bronchial tubes and quelled abdominal impurities and poisons. Some believed that one day a means of extracting the very essence of garlic would be discovered, helping to restore man's long-lost youth.

Alongside fruits and vegetables, aromatic and medicinal herbs were also grown in monastery gardens. Wild plants that monks had collected from nature gradually took root and settled in these gardens. Parsley, for instance, was cultivated in monasteries for medicine as well as seasoning in food. Every medieval monastery and convent had its own medically trained members versed in the field of herbs and treatment of illnesses. The most famous healer and expert on herbs in the high Middle Ages was Abbess Hildegard (1098–1179) of the convents of Rupertsberg and Eibingen.

Savoury and Sweet

Salt played an essential part in the medieval kitchen, mainly because it enabled the preservation of food. Both meat and fish were salted in order to be on hand throughout the year. When the salted product was eventually used, the excess salt would be soaked away to render it fit for consumption. The fondness for richly salted food among people in the Middle Ages has sometimes been exaggerated.

Salt was rarely added separately to food being cooked, especially if a stock that already contained enough salt was used, or the desired impact could be achieved with other ingredients, such as herbs. However, an individual salt cellar was an essential part of a table setting. Food ought not to be dipped directly into the salt;

rather, salt was to be retrieved with the tip of the knife. According to conduct books, dipping three fingers into the salt cellar was the sign of a peasant or an oaf.

Good-quality salt was not particularly cheap. Only pure white mineral salt would do as table salt for the Italian upper classes, and in England, too, the salt served at table needed to be white, dry and finely ground. From the mid-fourteenth century onwards, changes in the economy and the Hundred Years War led to a salt crisis, and the English were forced, more than ever before, to resort to poor-quality sea salt.

In the Middle Ages food was sweetened with sugar and honey. Dried fruits such as currants, raisins, dates, figs and prunes could also sweeten a dish, as could sweet-flavoured spices. There were several types of sugar, of which the cheapest varieties were likely to contain not insignificant amounts of impurities. Sugar added sweetness to drinks, breads and pastries, and it was also used to glaze or candy fruits, spices and confectionery. Moreover, it was needed to make marzipan. Sugar could be sprinkled onto sweet and savoury dishes, even onto sausages and the entrails of fish, before serving. As previously mentioned, a sweet flavour was often combined with some other flavour, particularly a sour one, in the Middle Ages.

Up until the high medieval era, sugar was a rare and expensive commodity reserved mainly for medicinal purposes. Only at the time of the Crusades did it become better known, appearing regularly for sale in European market towns from the fourteenth century onwards. In the late Middle Ages sugar was often the target of the prevailing sumptuary laws, becoming a mainstream product only in the early eighteenth century.

58 Bees and honey pictured in Biblioteca Casanatense's manuscript version of the *Tacuinum,* the *Theatrum sanitatis* (1400). Honey-glazed fruits were commonly served in monasteries, and honey was also needed as an ingredient in mead. Every prominent monastery kept its own beehives. Bees were tended throughout Europe for their honey, in addition to which the peasants capitalized on the honey reserves that wild bees accumulated. As honey was produced locally or at home, it rarely appeared in any purchasing ledgers.

Sugar was added to all types of food, as experts regarded it as having extremely warm and dry properties. It was thought to be one of the safest and most suitable of all ingredients. Certain Italian recipe collections suggested including sugar in almost half of their cooking instructions. In this book, too, sugar is included in many recipes, not excepting savoury dishes.

Sugar has been part of the inventories of pharmacists since time immemorial, and has appeared in almost every medieval medical drug and potion. It alleviated just about every ailment, and was of benefit to the healthy as well. Sugar cleansed the body and was good for the kidneys, blood and bladder. It was well suited to every temperament, age group, season and place.

In northern Europe all sugar had to be bought from abroad at great expense. England, for example, imported sugar from Syria, Rhodes, Alexandria and Sicily, although Cypriot sugar was thought to be the very finest. Late medieval Italy, on the other hand, already grew sugar in its own back yard, as the Arabs had established sugar cane in the southern part of the country. As sugar became increasingly common, it was used to create edible works of art with ever-growing

59 In medieval society the spice merchant and apothecary was a respected individual. Several years of apprenticeship and training had to be performed in order to achieve the title of apothecary. In cities the spice merchant's shop would be situated next to the cloth merchant, goldsmith and innkeeper. The spice merchant's place was a paradise of wondrous fragrances, where spices were stored in clay pots or bespoke containers. The clerk dispensed merchandise either by weight or by piece, and had to keep careful count of each sale.

regularity, and Venice, renowned for its sugar-refining trade, exported sugar sculptures to other parts of Italy. Marzipan made from sugar and almonds worked brilliantly as a component in the popular food structures of the era, although it could be eaten on its own as well. In 1460, by virtue of the laws on luxury, marzipan was banned at Venetian banquets. English master chefs, too, moulded images of the guests of honour and their castles from coloured marzipan. Their inspiration came from France, where marzipan had been produced from sugar and either pistachio nuts or almonds from the fourteenth century. Marzipan was originally an Arabian invention.

Honey was used in great quantities in medieval cooking to sweeten food and drink, particularly in England, Germany and the Nordic countries. Because sugar was expensive, a fair amount of honey was used in upper-class kitchens, too, particularly in northern regions at the end of the Middle Ages. In Italy the wealthy gradually lost interest in honey as sugar-refining intensified in the north Italian city states. However, the learned praised the beneficial properties of honey, affirming that it cleansed the chest and stomach and warmed the blood. It was particularly suited to those of cold and moist temperament. According to Mikael Agricola, honey drinks were appropriate above all in the month of March. 'You can live free of ache, if you my counsel take', he wrote, going on to advise the reader, in verse, that heads should not be bled in March, whereas frequent bathing was recommended, particularly when the weather turned hot. People could eat and drink whatever they pleased, in moderation. Furthermore food should be sweet, and drink thickened with honey.

Rue and pennyroyal, too, could be mixed to the brew, or cooked in the stew. And it was indeed beneficial to bathe a lot, although the bathwater should not be scalding hot. Finally, the main artery was not to be cupped, nor the principal vein of the thumb.

60 A man carrying curd, from the *Tacuinum sanitatis*.

seven

A SELECTION OF CHEESES: MILK AND EGG DISHES

In the Middle Ages the consumption of animal milk and milk-containing dishes was banned during the days of fasting determined by the Church. At other times, too, medieval chefs often resorted to cooking with 'milk' derived from almonds, from which long-lasting butter could also be made without using salt.

Most fresh animal milk was either used immediately in food preparation or transformed into salted milk products with a long shelf life. Animal milk was not chilled, and as a result it spoiled quickly and had to be used close to the source. The author of the French *Vivendier* culinary manuscript cautioned chefs to trust only milk that came to them directly from the cow. Milk vendors who peddled their wares in the city streets were often suspected of having diluted their product with water.

Milk was used as a cooking liquid for vegetables, and to moisten dough when baking. Various types of grain, rice and pasta could also be cooked in milk. Plain animal milk was only drunk for health reasons, and it was mostly recommended for children, adolescents and the feeble. In the Nordic countries everybody, including the healthy, drank buttermilk or other soured milk drinks of similar nature. Medical experts believed

animal milk to be nutritious, since its distinctive properties resembled those of the human body. Goat's and sheep's milk in particular were considered extremely beneficial. According to Mikael Agricola's book of prayers (*Rucouskiria*, 1544), people were well advised to drink both types, especially in the months of September and October. Cow's milk was thought to be difficult to digest, and was therefore recommended tempered with honey, pepper and wine.

The use of milk evolved in the cool regions of the North, where cow's milk was of greater significance than in the South. In the South stronger-tasting sheep's or goat's milk was predominantly consumed. The amount of milk derived from poor people's small cattle was particularly meagre. In the winter the cows were mostly unproductive, and the little milk that they produced was by preference used to make butter and cheese. Mikael Agricola maintained that fresh butter should be consumed especially in the month of May, when, after the long, northern winter, it was obviously more readily available. Butter churned in the autumn was exceptionally salty and long-lasting, although it did not necessarily remain in farmhouses, but was taken to town to be sold. The cream skimmed off the surface of milk was an important

61 The Devil helps the mistress of the house to milk somebody else's cow and churn the stolen milk in this mural painting from St Lawrence in the Finnish town of Lohja. A similar fresco can be found in Ösmo church in Sweden. In the Nordic countries women tended the dairy cattle and other domestic animals of the household. Pigs and hens roamed freely around the farmyard looking for feed. Cows, sheep and goats were milked mainly in the summer; in the winter they had to be put on a meagre diet. Milk was soured into buttermilk or churned into butter or cheese. Fresh milk was set aside for children and the infirm; others drank watered-down buttermilk or *kalja*, a type of small beer, with their meals. Butter was an expensive treat, and only a tiny lump was spread on bread on special occasions. The Häme and Turku Castle account books from the early modern period show entries for milk, buttermilk, eggs, cheese and butter.

ingredient in many fine foods, such as the English cream pie with raisins and dates.

Cheeses for Every Palate

Cheese was extremely popular in the Middle Ages. It had many uses, and in warm regions in particular, a long-lasting cheese was the most usable of all milk products. Many cheeses that we know today were familiar already in the Middle Ages. Cheese belonged everywhere and at every meal, and not just as an accompaniment, as is often the case today. For periods of fasting, cheeses in all but name were made from almond milk and fish stock for the tables of the upper classes.

Cows were important animals in medieval monasteries, and many monasteries were well-known cheese producers. Monks rarely drank plain milk, but cheese was consumed in abundance. Peasants living in mountain and cattle-raising regions also knew the noble art of cheese-making. Many monasteries owned large landholdings, which they leased to peasants as summer pasturage. In Germany peasants could rent alpine huts and grassland complete with cheese pans and other tools for making cheese and butter all summer long. The rent was paid in cheese: large, landowning monasteries could receive as many as tens of thousands of cheeses at the end of one summer. The monks also undertook journeys to bless the fields and cattle of the peasants, for which they received large cheeses in reward.

In upper-class food preparation mature cheese was used mainly in soups and bakery products. The process of cheese making yielded a milk-like liquid for cooking, and fresh, or unripened, cheeses were well suited to adding to a large number of pastries.

Cheeses were divided into hard, soft and fresh cheeses. Hard cheeses were made from whole milk and dried into wheels, while soft cheeses were made from semi-skimmed milk

62 Men carrying a good-sized cake of cheese in a woodcut from Olaus Magnus's work. Cheese was the stuff of fairy tales. Known far and wide is the age-old fable of the fox and the raven. The raven, prone to gluttony, was also susceptible to praise, while the cunning fox mastered the art of flattery to perfection. The raven had seized a piece of cheese and taken it high up in a tree to feast on. The fox began to flatter the raven, enticing it to sing. When the raven opened its beak to oblige, the cheese fell to the ground. The fox grabbed the cheese and devoured it. The moral of the story is that he that is wise does not fall for flattery and honeyed words, which cause nothing but trouble.

and used before hardening. Fresh, unripened cheeses were similar to the curd and whey cheeses we know today. According to medieval medical science, young, immature cheese was cold and moist, and should therefore be used with caution. Well-aged, mature cheese was warmer, albeit dry – partly due to its salt content – and therefore it, too, had to be used carefully. Medium-aged cheese was the safest.

In Italy cheese was used generously and in many and various ways in cooking. Just like today, it was recommended particularly with pasta. Hard cheese was ground and added to bakery products, soups and sausage filling. Among the best-liked cheeses was Parmesan, for which there was a market abroad as well. Low cost cheeses were available to the poor.

The French, too, rated cheese highly. The late fourteenth-century author of the *Ménagier de Paris* collection even put together a rhyming checklist of the signs of a good cheese:

Non mye blanc comme Helayne,
Non mye pleurant comme Magdalaine,
Non Argus, maiz du tout aveugle . . .
Tigneulx, rebelle, bien pesant

In other words, a good cheese was not pale like Helen of Troy or weeping like Mary Magdalene, nor was it multi-eyed like Argus, the Greek mythological giant with a hundred eyes; it would be hard-rinded, firm and weighty.

Often cheese was eaten plain, together with a piece of bread or some dried fruit. Fourme d'Ambert cheese was flavoured with nuts, almonds, dried figs and raisins. Honey-flavoured, slowly maturing blue cheeses were popular.

The Grouping of Courses from a Nutritive Point of View

The grouping of courses and the dishes these comprised, particularly when it came to formal entertaining among the upper classes, was based on the opinions of health guides. To secure the proper absorption of food, it was important to take into account the order in which different dishes were best consumed, as an impeded digestion was thought to have horrific consequences. The digestive process was perceived to be similar to the ripening process, and it was therefore a big mistake to eat ricotta cheese, for instance, at the beginning of a meal. Foods on which the 'human oven' had to work long and hard to assimilate into nutrition were to be eaten towards the end of a repast.

The aperitif 'opened' a person's stomach — the term comes from the Latin *aperire*, 'to open'. It could be either solid or liquid, so long as its distinctive properties helped the rest of the food to travel down to the stomach, promoting good digestion. Wine, taken in reasonable quantities on an empty stomach, opened the abdomen and awakened the appetite. Fruits were suitable first courses — particularly peaches, although melons, cherries, strawberries and grapes were also satisfactory — and so were lettuce with oil and vinegar, cabbage, soft-boiled eggs and honey — or sugar-sweetened confectionery with anise, caraway or pine nuts.

Now the stomach was prepared to receive the succeeding courses. First, easily digested, light meat such as chicken and baby goat was served, and simmered dishes such as vegetable or meat stews. Indeed most broths and soups were offered at the beginning of a meal, at which stage the author of the *Ménagier de Paris* (1392–4) also recommended items such as spiced wine, tartlets and pasties, stewed leeks, beans and vegetables, meat cooked in almond milk, soups and apple turnovers.

After this, heavy fruits such as pears and chestnuts, and heavy meat such as ox and pork, were appropriate suggestions, as were roasted joints with their respective sauces. The last main course might include game or fish dishes. In the event that fish was served, nuts were to be offered immediately afterwards, since they were dry and neutralized excess moisture. If, on the other hand, meat was served, roots or fruits were fine alternatives to follow, or cheese that was not too aged and dry.

After the meal, the stomach had to be 'sealed' and warmed a second time with a suitable digestive. Various sweet, oven-baked items and crêpes that were either sugar-glazed or filled with sweet custard cream were recommended when getting up from table, as were light cakes, candied fruits, ginger, cinnamon and coriander confectionery and spiced drinks, of which hippocras was by far the best known. Owing to its superb digestive qualities, sugar belonged to both the beginning and the end of a meal. Fruit was served in sugar or honey syrup, or puréed into sweet, spiced pulp. Fruits could be either fresh or dried, like prunes and raisins, so long as the spiced sweetmeats offered at the end of the meal promoted good digestion, while simultaneously rendering the breath of the diners pleasantly fresh-smelling.

63 Ricotta cheese-makers at work in an illustration from the *Tacuinum sanitatis* (1474).

Roquefort, for instance, made from sheep's milk, is still a familiar cheese today.

St Marcellin was a small, round cheese made famous by a certain incident involving Louis XI of France. One day the King was hunting in Vercors and came upon a bear. Alerted by his cries for help, some brave woodcutters first saved the King and then offered him their bread and cheese. So delighted was the King by the flavour of the cheese, which was mild, tangy, salty and nutty, that he elevated his saviours to the nobility then and there. In the Middle Ages St Marcellin cheese was made from goat's milk, although cow's milk is mostly used these days.

A favourite among cheese pies was the *flamiche au maroilles*, also served at elegant upper-class banquets. Maroilles was a light-coloured soft cheese made from cow's milk, strong-flavoured without being sharp. A gingered cheese pie made with Brie was widely popular too.

Eggs: A Ubiquitous All-rounder

Eggs were used in great abundance and with much creativity in the Middle Ages. Every peasant kept a coop with hens and roosters, and many townspeople raised a hen or two for eggs. Chicken eggs were popular, and goose eggs an even greater delicacy. The wealthy also valued

64 A cheese merchant's shop. The illustrator has depicted on the counter a measuring beam, with a sliding weight, and a sharp knife with which the cheese was cut.

cordo psalterio: cum cantico

65 A woman feeding a hen and chicks, in an illustration from the *Luttrell Psalter*.

66 Toll on markets levied by a cleric, 15th century.

partridge, pheasant, duck and dove eggs. Peahen and ostrich eggs were neither common nor considered very palatable

Monasteries, too, raised poultry, and eggs – particularly chicken eggs – were eaten and used in cooking in staggering quantities, judging from the information that remains with us today. At Cluny Abbey in France, in the high medieval era, the permitted daily allowance was 30 eggs per person – a number that may appear astonishing to modern readers. A certain English abbot is said to have proposed that the limit be drawn at a maximum of 55 eggs at a time. As stated in the fifteenth-century ledgers of a Winchester monastery, a family of 30 would partake of 400 eggs in the first course of a meal during a period of fasting, followed by salmon, cod and sardines. Eggs went down well with the folk of the Nordic countries, too, low and high alike: according to the ledgers at the Turku Castle

court of Duke John, in 1563 no less than 17,208 chicken eggs were consumed.

The popularity of the egg lay in its many uses. Medieval recipe collections included a number of cooking instructions that involved eggs; similarly eggs are included in many of the recipes collected for this book, either as supplements to or main ingredients in a dish. In the medieval kitchen eggs were used for thickening soups and sauces, binding pastries and jellies, and making cheese. In separate egg dishes the eggs could be boiled, stuffed, fried, cooked *en cocotte*, poached, stewed or whipped into an omelette that was either plain or flavoured with cheese and herbs. For special occasions laborious and expensive egg dishes such as baked goose stuffed with eggs or egg stew with peppercorns, honey and saffron could be prepared. Egg cheese was served for dessert at elegant banquets, together with grapes, raisins, almonds and cakes.

Good and Bad Table Manners

Just like today, in the Middle Ages there were both those who were foul and badly behaved and those who appreciated and observed cleanliness and decorum, at table as well as elsewhere. Alongside chronicles — such as the work of the French poet and historiographer Jean Molinet, which provides an in-depth account of the strict dining etiquette at the Burgundian court — contemporary handbooks on behaviour also shed some light on the customs and rules pertaining to eating. Guides to good manners were issued throughout the Middle Ages. The early twelfth-century Latin-language *Disciplina clericalis* by Petrus Alphonsi was one of the earliest publications, while Erasmus of Rotterdam's 1530 treatise on good manners for boys, *De civilitate morum puerilium*, which he dedicated to young Henry of Burgundy, was among the better known.

Erasmus's directives on table manners are manifold and traditional, focusing the attention on cleanliness, calm and restraint. 'To fidget around in your seat, and to settle first on one buttock and then the next, gives the impression that you are repeatedly emitting wind, or trying to do so . . . Some people, no sooner than they have sat down, immediately stick their hands into the dishes of food. This is the manner of wolves.' The diner was not to help himself to every dish presented, but to settle for whatever was in front of him. If one selection seemed irresistible, it was polite to leave part or all of it to somebody else.

Swallowing the food whole was to copy storks or jesters, while wolfing it down was for thieves. The food was not to be crammed into the mouth all at once, causing the cheeks to puff out like bellows. 'Some, when they chew, open their jaws so wide that they grunt like pigs. Others, again, when they swallow, breathe through their noses so hard that they appear to be choking', Erasmus wrote. Talking with one's mouth full of food was neither polite nor safe.

Uninterrupted eating and drinking gave the impression of mental impairment, as did scratching the head, picking the teeth, toying with the fork, gesticulating, coughing, hawking and spitting at table — although could it be that behaviour of this sort only stemmed from a provincial lack of confidence?

While at table it was advisable to take a break from eating every now and then and devote oneself to conversation. However, in the event that one had to sit and listen to the talk of others without getting a chance to participate, all signs of boredom ought to be carefully concealed. It was rude to sit at table lost in one's own thoughts, or to let one's gaze wander. The very worst behaviour was to turn one's head and sneak a look at what was going on at the next table.

Bones and other food scraps were not to be thrown beneath the table, littering the floor, nor were they to be swept onto the tablecloth — not to mention depositing them back onto the serving platter. Instead they ought to be arranged along the edge of the diner's own plate, or placed in a dish expressly reserved for leftovers. To offer food from the table to other people's dogs was tactless, and to pet the dogs during the course of the meal was even more inconsiderate.

Being morose and spreading misery among the other diners was ill-mannered. Gaiety

67 Good and bad table manners are illustrated in a 15th-century manuscript of Valerius Maximus' *Memorabilia*.

should characterize a festive meal, although not in an exaggeratedly ebullient or unruly fashion. Nothing that might put a damper on the atmosphere should be said. It was wrong to deride those who were not present, or those who, due to lack of experience, made a faux pas during the course of the festivities. Similarly it was impolite and unappreciative towards the host to seek fault with what was served. Good manners called for the host himself to apologize for the modest nature of the event. Praising one's own table and calling attention to the cost ruined the appetite of the invited guests.

The meticulous enumeration of bad manners in conduct books does not prove that they were rife. Teaching methods, particularly in the late Middle Ages, tended to emphasize the negative aspects of things, subscribing to tactics of incrimination and intimidation. To give an example, teachings on the hereafter focused in much greater detail on hellfire and damnation than on paradise and all that was good. Contrary to what is commonly believed, good table manners were both appreciated and observed in the Middle Ages, and therefore given much consideration. Efforts were made to teach children acceptable behaviour from an early age, since dining was a communal event that took place far more frequently back then than today. ⌫

68 The five senses are the main theme of *The Lady and the Unicorn* tapestry, made for Jean Le Viste, a courtier of King Charles VII. In the piece dedicated to the sense of taste, the pennants and the armours of the unicorn and the lion bear the arms of the patron. The Lady is taking a sweet from the candy dish offered to her by a servant. At her feet a monkey is eating a berry or a sweet, underlining the message of the scene. In the medieval hierarchy of senses, sight was in the top position, followed by hearing, smell, taste and touch. The senses were seen as essential instruments for acquiring understanding, but they were also viewed as dangerous weapons capable of leading man astray, into temptation and sin.

eight

DIVINE DESSERTS

Many of the desserts and sweet pastries that we know today were already familiar in the Middle Ages. Having said that, missing from the selection of sweet delights were chocolate and other items flavoured with cocoa and vanilla. Puddings and jellies lent themselves well to being desserts, such as the festive, two-coloured almond milk pudding, a sweet course that Master Chef Taillevent served his royal patrons and their guests in late fourteenth-century France.

As we discovered earlier, sweet delicacies and pastries belonged not only to the beginning of a festive meal, but also, and in fact first and foremost, to the later courses. On getting up from table, hippocras (a spiced wine) together with light pastries was ingested. This might be followed by gingered confectionery and other dainties served in a separate room.

Tantalizing Treats

Many medieval cakes and sweet pastries were identified with various religious orders, since monasteries turned out great quantities of baked goods. Some former favourites have since disappeared, for instance *bernardins*, which were produced by an order of the same name and soon became a popular purchase among pilgrims. At church entrances and in conjunction with religious feasts, monks often distributed small, dry cakes or crispy biscuits to the faithful, still known today in France as *craquelins*, *macarons* and *massepains*. *Nonettes*, or 'young nuns', were small, round spice cakes, while oblong *sacristains*, or 'sextons', from Provence were made from puff pastry rolled in crystal sugar. The jocularly named *pets-de-nonne* ('nun's farts') or *soupirs de nonne* ('nun's sighs') were pastries filled with buttercream.

The dough of the popular *oublyes* biscuits was similar to that of the sacramental wafer. These biscuits were also served at monastery suppers, particularly at Easter and on certain other feast days. The sacramental wafer was intended to illustrate the purity of Christ, and was therefore a pure white colour, a requirement made clear by the Dominican theologian Thomas Aquinas in the thirteenth century. By using the most fine-meshed sieve available, white wheat flour was obtained, and sometimes chalk was even added to the batch to make it whiter.

Bibers (German for beavers) were made from flour, honey and almond paste, and were originally baked in German monasteries. It has been

69 In Gerard David's painting of a marriage feast, a servant brings in a cake, while the carver is shown in the act of carving the meat in front of the table. At medieval banquets it was not unusual to serve sweet delicacies and pastries together with savoury dishes. At a German feast, for instance, guests could enjoy roasted wildfowl in pepper sauce, sugar-sweetened rice, gingered trout, sugar-coated pancakes – and still some pastries to round off the third course. Particularly during Carnival, sweet bakery products, pancakes, crêpes and cakes flavoured with sugar, spices, nuts or candied fruits were indulged in throughout Europe.

suggested that today's ginger snaps were also initially developed in a German monastery. Various biscuits were baked for commerce as well. These were rarely used in cooking – in other words, they were not crumbled – and therefore needed to have a long shelf life.

Waffles, too, were for sale in great quantities, since, besides being eaten as such, they could be used as the top or bottom layer of a pie. On saints' days waffle- and pastry-vendors in big cities pushed ovens on wheels, hawking their freshly baked wares to passers-by. In France these street traders were so important and well liked that they separated from the professional confectioners' guild and formed their own. Waffles, crêpes, pancakes and fritters were popular not just among the lower classes, but with the wealthy as well. The court of Edward IV of England (1442–1483) employed a special waffle-maker,

and at English upper-class banquets waffles could be served throughout the meal.

Fritters, or deep-fried pastries similar to crêpes or pancakes, were another variety of pastry. The batter was made from flour and eggs. In Italy fritters were often sweet. Sugar and rose water were used as flavouring, and different fruits were recommended as fillings. Herbs, flowers and fresh cheese could also be deep-fried, while savoury fritters often involved fish or fish roe. In Italy and England yeast was sometimes also used in fritters, an ingredient rarely used in other pastries. In England beer was often added to the batter, while fruits, root vegetables and fresh cheese were common choices for deep-frying.

Fritters were fried in oil and eaten with sugar or honey. *Cryspes*, comparable to funnel cakes, were fatty speciality pastries of a similar nature.

Fruity Temptations

In the Middle Ages fruits, nuts and berries were part of the diet of every social order, and the most readily available varieties were also the ones most commonly consumed. Pineapples, coconuts and kiwi fruit, all present-day favourites, had not yet found their way to Europe, and bananas, although known, were shunned. Fresh, sugar-glazed and dried fruits were eaten at both the beginning and the end of a meal. At the royal courts of England the person in charge of pastries and spices also handled the procurement of suitable fruits from the royal gardens, appropriately tailored for the occasion and the time of year. Even the poor had access to fruit, and in day-to-day life children were rewarded with fruits and nuts.

70 Woman carrying a fruit tray, in a detail from a fresco by Domenico Ghirlandaio (1449–1494). Heedless of the theories and warnings issued by physicians and other learned men, apples, pears, peaches, plums, cherries, figs, dates and raisins were also served and eaten fresh and unprocessed. Different types of fruit were sold in large quantities, having been picked in the wild or raised in orchards and gardens.

At upper-class dinners fruit, nuts and berries often had a supplemental role. Fruits were served as separate components of a meal, and also in conjunction with various prepared dishes. On festive occasions fruit and vegetable compotes were offered with meat or fish, eaten cold as a salad. Fruit was generally taken at a relatively early stage of a formal meal, or during the third course, and possibly again as a last course immediately following dessert. Young, or unripe, fruit was not recommended, as the medical experts thought it hard to digest. If unripe fruit was served, it had to be accompanied by ingredients believed to have counter-indicative, digestive effects, for instance hippocras, hard cheese, nuts or sugared spices.

For a long time, the choice of fruit depended on the time of the year. The greatest selection was to be had in late summer during the ripening season; an opportune time for the poor, too, to avail themselves of the most common varieties. Long-distance shipping of fruit was time-consuming and expensive, and storage was difficult as well.

Citrus fruits, figs, dates and pomegranates were most readily available in the temperate countries around the Mediterranean Sea. They were traded elsewhere, too, although were rarely used by anybody but the very rich in the Nordic countries. Figs were exported as far as the Baltic region, as were raisins, dates and citrus fruits. The latter were not eaten on their own, but squeezed for their juice, which was used to flavour pastries, fish dishes and sauces. The cultivation of apples, pears, quinces, plums and grapes, on the other hand, was widespread throughout Europe. England supplemented its

71 Adam, Eve, apples and the snake in Paradise in a painting by Hugo van der Goes. In the Middle Ages apples were the most commonly eaten fruits. They were readily available, since apple trees grew wild in fields. The apple, particularly the apple of the Tree of Knowledge in the Garden of Eden, was the symbol of temptation and original sin. In many medieval religious illustrations the apple that led to the fall of Adam and Eve was pictured in the mouth of a snake. In some paintings the Christ Child is depicted as grasping an apple, thus taking upon himself the sins of the world. The sweet taste of the apple was also interpreted as a sign of temptation. In non-spiritual allegory the apple was by virtue of its shape a cosmic emblem: alongside the sceptre, rulers often brandished 'an imperial apple' portraying the earth. Already in antiquity the pomegranate had found its way to the regions around the Mediterranean Sea through the conveyance of the Phoenicians. Because it was filled with seeds, it soon became a symbol of fruitfulness. In Christian allegory it was declared a sign of divine blessing and heavenly love, and the red juice of the fruit was seen as an allusion to the blood that was shed by martyrs.

fruit reserves by importing from Holland and France.

Alexander the Great had brought peaches and apricots to Europe around 300 BC. By then, peach and apricot trees had already been cultivated in China for thousands of years. Peaches, or 'Persian plums' (*Prunus persica*), were greatly appreciated in the late Middle Ages. In medieval Christian iconography the peach symbolized the Holy Trinity, salvation and truth. The Greeks and the Romans nicknamed the apricot 'the golden egg of the sun'. The apricot is related to the peach, plum, cherry, almond and bitter almond. In northern Europe the cultivation of apricots began only in the sixteenth century.

The poor knew apples and pears best. At the tables of the gentry, intricate sweet and savoury dishes were prepared from these fruits, which were also used as decoration. In addition they could be juiced for food preparation, in which case the liquid was applied in the same way as vinegar. Cider was also made from apples. The English created apple accompaniments to supplement their meat dishes, and the Germans braised apples in butter to serve with savoury main dishes on elegant occasions. Baking apples in hot ashes was a popular pastime in winter. Pears were often poached in a sugared solution fortified with wine, frequently containing honey and cinnamon as well.

Initially plants were left to grow more or less wild, until, in the late Middle Ages, increased attention was given to the care of fruit trees and garden plants. Commercial cultivation and tending of gardens developed as a result of the help and support of the lay and ecclesiastical upper classes and the newly rich bourgeoisie,

and an increased general familiarity with recently discovered tastes. Italy was considered a pioneer in the field of gardening, and among the novel species at hand, citrus fruits, for instance, were established in southern Italy in the high medieval era.

Since it was difficult to store fresh fruit, and medical experts did not recommend eating uncooked fruit, fruits were often processed in one way or another. Poaching in a sugar-sweetened solution or making jams or purées was a popular alternative, as sugar and honey neutralized harmful distinctive properties and guaranteed a long shelf life. A syrup-like reduction of red wine also enabled fruit to be preserved. Fruits were used liberally in the preparation of sauces and food pastry, and were also pan-fried or spit-roasted over an open fire.

As noted, the use of dried fruits – raisins, currants, prunes, dates and figs – was common. According to medical experts, dried fruits were recommendable for different fillings, pastries and meat dishes, because they preserved moisture and sweetened the food. Dried fruits were also made into their own soups and dishes, for instance *hasteletes of fruyt*, or spit-roasted fruits, which were suitable for periods of fasting.

Plums were grown in China more than 4,000 years ago. In the Far East the plum symbolized springtime and youth. The fruit was known in antiquity, but did not become permanently established in western Europe until the time of the Crusades. Medieval monasteries maintained vast plum orchards, and new species were enthusiastically developed in, for instance, sixteenth-century France. Only in the seventeenth century were plum trees established in Finland.

In the medieval kitchen dried plums, or prunes, were used in a number of dishes, although plums were also eaten fresh. On the authority of the fifteenth-century Italian scholar Bartolomeo Platina, plums were considered excellent starters, since they eased and improved the function of the bowels, warmed the bile and quelled the thirst. In medieval Christian iconography the plum was often a sign of devotion, although it could acquire different meanings depending on its colour. In imagery describing the different stages of the life of Christ, a purple plum indicated the suffering and death of the Redeemer, while a golden-yellow plum stood for virtue and a red one for brotherly love.

The region where the date palm first appeared has not been identified precisely, although the tree has been known for at least 3,000 years. The date palm grows in dry, subtropical climates, particularly near oases. The flavour of the fully developed date is sweet and honeyed, although not as sugary as when dried. Fresh dates do not keep well and are rarely available in northern regions, but dried dates can be obtained throughout the year.

The fig, on the other hand, has its origin in Asia Minor. Nowadays fig trees are widely cultivated in tropical and subtropical regions. The flavour of a ripened fig is sweet with just a hint of sour, and dried figs are sweeter still. In medieval art the fig tree often appeared in paintings of Paradise, where Adam and Eve wore nothing but fig leaves. In antiquity the fig tree was, in addition to the grapevine, the emblem of Dionysus, originally the Greek god of fertility and later of wine (Roman Bacchus), and also of Priapus, a minor

god of fertility with a huge and permanently erect phallus. It was thought in the Middle Ages that the Latin word *peccare*, 'to sin', came from *pag*, the Hebrew word for 'fig'. An insult known in all of Europe was the obscene *mano fica* (fig hand) gesture. In Christian symbolism, 'the withered fig tree' stood for Judaism or heresy (compare Matthew 21:19), whereas, conversely, a fruit-bearing fig tree signified halcyon days in the heavenly kingdom.

Strawberry Red and Blueberry Blue

In the Middle Ages berries were used rather in the same way as fruits, although they had an even shorter shelf life. When dried, berries of course remained usable for much longer. It is believed that berries were used less frequently in upper-class food preparation than fruits, although with nothing but cooking instructions and ledger entries to go by, it is difficult to establish an accurate view of the matter, since freshly eaten products were rarely entered into journals and written manuscripts as conscientiously as other foods.

Recent archaeological research indicates that wild berries played an important part in the Nordic food industry. In the Baltic region the most common species was the raspberry, from the rose family, the actual cultivation of which began in the sixth century. Blackcurrants and redcurrants were not used in any significant quantities until the late Middle Ages. The cultivation of blackcurrants began in northern France, Flanders and the northern parts of continental Europe, from where it spread to England. The cultivation of redcurrants got under way in Central Europe in

72 Strawberries, raspberries, currants and cherries symbolize sensual pleasure and the corruption of virtues in Hieronymus Bosch's painting. However, in depictions of Paradise, the Virgin Mary and the baby Jesus, berries often had positive meanings. Although never mentioned in the Bible, the strawberry was generally regarded as a paradisal berry. Its three-lobed leaves alluded to the Holy Trinity and its white flower to innocence and humility, while the red berry referred to the sufferings and death of Christ. Yet some medieval scholars were of the opinion that the higher a fruit grew, the nobler it was; and on these grounds there was reason to regard low-growing plants such as the strawberry with suspicion.

73 A customer examining a fig seller's produce in a 15th-century miniature by Évrard d'Espinques. From Bartholomeus Anglicus, *On the Properties of Things* (*De proprietatibus rerum*).

the sixteenth century, and both species spread to Scandinavia in the seventeenth century. In Finland the oldest cultivated types of currants are the 'Red Dutch' and 'White Dutch' varieties, which are mentioned in publicized texts from 1665.

Archaeological sources from the Baltic region also reveal the existence of strawberries, blueberries, rowanberries and cherries, although these are hardly ever mentioned in written texts. Archaeological excavations on the small island of Helgeandsholmen in Stockholm have unearthed damson, plum, apple, fig and cherry seeds, together with the seeds of sloes, bird cherries, rose hips, raspberries, strawberries, cloudberries and blueberries, and hazelnuts and walnuts.

The positive effects of berries on general health were soon established. Hildegard of Bingen (1098–1179) recommended sloes for a number of complaints. Since ancient times bacciferous, or berry-bearing, plants had been used for their therapeutic qualities in the treatment of gallstones, coughs, tuberculosis and other inflammations. Modern research has produced ample scientific evidence of the positive effects that wild berries have on general health. Cranberries, for instance, have proved successful in preventing inflammation of the urinary tract.

English cookery books mention blackberries, strawberries and rose hips, all of which could be cooked in wine. Almond milk was also a suitable cooking liquid for berry recipes. Strawberries and cherries could be used with meat as well — the former in dishes such as bone marrow pies, a combination that may seem bizarre to us today. Strawberries were available both in the wild and from gardens, where they were established in the twelfth or thirteenth centuries. (Today's large, garden-grown strawberries, *Fragaria x ananassa,* have only been cultivated since the nineteenth century.) Although medical experts did not recommend eating unprocessed berries for health reasons, fresh strawberries, for instance, were nevertheless enjoyed as such even at sophisticated events. In the summer of 1497, at a banquet held by the Goldsmiths' Guild in London, fresh strawberries with sugar were served with every course.

The odd reference to wild berries is made in Celtic and Irish mythology. In one ancient tale Branwen, the daughter of Llyr and Penarddun and the goddess of love and beauty, transforms herself into a wild strawberry. In ancient Finnish folklore blueberries and wild strawberries can lure a picker astray; alternatively they may possess magic powers. Berries also inspired songs, poetry, proverbs and parables. The phrase 'sour grapes' was coined in one of Aesop's fables (*c.* 620–560 BC), although in most Western translations the grapes were changed to sour berries. In Finland they became rowanberries. The fox in the fable vainly coveted the berries in a tree and finally, admitting failure, declared them sour and withdrew in disappointment from the effort. The moral of the story was that man tends to find fault with what he cannot have himself. But rowanberries are indeed sour, and in the Nordic countries they were made into a wine-like drink in the Middle Ages.

Nuts to Crack

Nut plants, too, played an important part in the medieval diet. Peanuts were not yet known, whereas walnuts, hazelnuts, pistachio nuts, pine nuts, chestnuts and almonds were permanently on hand in large medieval kitchens. As for the price of nuts, it could actually be quite high – but the kernels made fine ingredients in both sweet and savoury specialities.

In Italy nut oil was a cherished type of food oil. A type of milk was also made from nuts (*latte di noce*), although it was less commonly used than almond milk. In England, too, nuts were transformed into nut milk. Walnuts and hazelnuts were also part of the food culture around the Baltic Sea. Archaeological research has unearthed walnuts from fourteenth-century Finland.

Chestnuts were a staple for common people in medieval France, among other places. The nuts were eaten on their own, and also together with meat and fish, or ground into flour. In October the peasants organized harvest feasts, when fresh or roasted chestnuts were eaten. Plain, boiled chestnuts went well with a variety of foods, and the nuts could also be roasted or ground into flour. Despite being considered second-class, chestnuts are mentioned in Italian cookery books, although they do not appear in the English equivalents.

The fruit of the almond is not a real nut but a drupe – a fruit with a stone containing a seed. Almonds in particular were unparalleled in importance in medieval food economies. Almonds had many uses, but were quite expensive. The almond tree requires a temperate climate for growing, and therefore did not do well in the North. The upper

74 A nutcracker with a human face. As far as symbols go, the nut enjoyed a most favourable rating in the Middle Ages, with its hard shell encasing a precious inner part. In tales and legends, nuts harboured within themselves many wondrous gifts. Augustine of Hippo (AD 354–430) saw the nutshell as representing the body of Christ, destined to endure bitter suffering, while the core of the fruit epitomized the divine communication that nourished the soul of man and enabled him, with the help of its oil, to see the light.

Sugared almonds were taken as a digestive at the end of a meal, as were other nuts.

Almond milk could be converted into various artificial milk products for days of fasting. Almond cheese and substitute butter and eggs are prime examples. One English recipe recommended blowing out the internal part of an egg through a hole and pouring a spiced concoction based on almond milk in its place, part of which had been tinted yellow with saffron. A certain skill was required to make the 'yolk' stay separate from the white, and eventually to bake the imitation egg without breaking it.

classes used almonds mostly for almond milk or almond cream, both of which were made from ground almonds and liquid. The Arabs had introduced the concept of almond milk, and they also used almond extract to thicken and flavour their sauces. Among Europeans, almond milk was a basic element in the dishes created for periods of fasting, although it was used liberally at other times as well.

Almonds were added shelled or blanched, ground or pan-fried to food. Blanched almonds were liked for their beautiful white colour, although shelled almonds were also used. Fried almonds were good for decorating dishes. Almonds could be sprinkled over a soup, cooked in wine or beer, or used for making marzipan. Menus were known to include separate almond dishes alongside the meat and fish dishes.

Visual Delights of the Table: Colours and Aesthetics

In the Middle Ages, an age when beauty was revered, pleasure was conveyed not only through taste, but also through visual perception. Opulence, aesthetics and symbolism were high on the list of priorities in upper-class food culture. Food was supposed to seduce the eye, and forms and colours were given careful attention. Dishes were put together in complicated arrangements according to a chosen theme, and decorated with religious or political symbols that could be further elaborated on with the help of texts and inscriptions. Tortellini and ravioli were cut into the shapes of horseshoes, rings, animals or letters. Meat and fish were encased in transparent aspic jellified into surprisingly complex forms. Piecrusts were decorated with images of historical or mythical themes set in dough. Gilded with saffron or egg yolk, they permitted the flamboyant presentation of any type of food ranging from vegetables to meat, while simultaneously offering an element of surprise. When it came to sauces, chefs played with colours to please the eye and stimulate the appetite of the diners. France's royal head chef Taillevent chose the colours of his sauces to coordinate with his cooking techniques: green sauce for poached fish, orange for grilled and brown for fried.

Bright, rich and vibrant colours were attempted in festive dishes in particular. Brightness was achieved by repeatedly straining the food through a sieve. Medieval culture adored colours, to which great symbolic significance was attached. A dish could be named according to its colour. A large selection of roots, plants, mushrooms, woods, minerals, herbs and spices was used for colouring, as were egg yolks and toasted bread.

A golden-yellow colour was primarily obtained from saffron, which was expensive. On the other hand, because of its excellent pigment, only a small amount of saffron was required to colour a full portion of food. The surface of a roast or pie could be given a handsome, smooth, glistening, golden-yellow crust with the help of saffron paste. Although not very common, genuine gold or silver leaf could also be used for coating. The least expensive way to create yellow was to use egg yolk.

White or light-coloured dishes often appeared on bills of fare, either for symbolic reasons or as a contrast to and departure from dark-coloured foods. White pudding, or medieval *blanc manger*, in which the key ingredient was almond milk, was a favoured dish on festive occasions. The colour green was achieved from parsley boiled in white wine or any other pale liquid. Green could also be derived from basil and spinach juice, mint, mallow, sorrel, wheatgrass and the leaves of nut trees. A greenish fluid for the colouring of sauces and pastries could be extracted from practically every kitchen herb.

Red was obtained from the juice of cherries and other red berries and grapes, and from rose petals, sandalwood and alkanet, or dyers' bugloss, to name just a few. Blue came from blueberries, columbine buds and cornflowers. Brown, again, was extracted from cinnamon and dried fruits such as raisins, and black from dark grapes, prunes, boiled chicken liver, blood and bread toasted dark.

75 A baked swan and the head of a wild boar brought to table are the highlights of the meal for these attending aristocrats. In medieval culture the white colour of the swan made it a symbol of purity and beauty. In England the head of a wild boar was known to be served at the feasts of Michaelmas and Christmas, namely at the royal table. The retrieval of certain parts of a boar, such as its testicles, was an entitlement reserved for the aristocracy, and this particular bounty belonged to the nobleman who had felled the beast.

Colour preferences varied. The Italian upper classes, for instance, favoured golden yellow, green and white. Picture sources and archaeological evidence show that emphasis was also put on yellow and white for table settings, by means of table linen, decorative arrangements and serving dishes fashioned from precious metals. Gold was popular in England, too, and red more so than in Italy – red and gold being the colours of the royal house of England. In medieval culture gold was generally the most highly regarded colour; then again, ordinary yellow was the least appreciated. In the late Middle Ages blue bypassed red in popularity, although this general drift undoubtedly involved fabrics rather than food trends.

Colour combinations were also common, and food could be multicoloured. In pastry fillings of differing colours could be applied in layers. Several colours could be presented on the same serving platter, either in dishes that had been dyed differently, or in one and the same dish divided into two fields of colour, a design known as a party pattern. Chequerboard patterns were also used. Fresh flowers such as roses, elderflowers, hawthorn blossoms, primroses and violets brought colour to both foods and table settings. On the whole, the food and its surroundings were expected to look exceptional at upper-class tables, and a rich assortment of colours was used. A festive meal was not just the sum of its food components, but one aesthetic whole, including the presentation of the dishes and the setting, music and spectacles, all alongside the quality of the food itself.

With its directions on how to build a pie castle, the *Forme of Cury* (*c.* 1390) provides us with an insight into how colours were used when creating food structures for the banquets of the gentry. First the foundation and towers are built from dough. The towers must be pre-baked in the oven. For the central tower, a saffron-gilded filling of pork and eggs is made, and for the surrounding towers, a filling of almond cream, milk and eggs coloured red with sandalwood. The assembled castle is then baked in the oven. An alternative filling for the towers can be prepared from a brown paste of figs, raisins, apples and pears. Green-coloured fruit pudding can also be used as a filling, if so desired.

76 Grapes are harvested beneath the castle walls, and on the other side of the lake, autumn fruits are picked from the trees in a miniature from the *Grimani Breviary*. Grapevines had been cultivated in Egypt and the Near East around 3000 BC. As monastic organizations spread throughout Europe with the progress of Christianity, the number of vineyards increased as well. Each monastery had its own plantation of grapevines, and wine-making became the most important means of generating an income. In Tuscany, the Rhine and Rhone Valleys, and in Champagne and Avignon, the most advanced wine-producing regions were situated around the bishoprics.

nine

OF HIPPOCRAS
AND MEAD

In medieval Europe coffee, tea and cocoa were unfamiliar products. Wine and beer were usually served at mealtimes. Plain water was rarely taken with food or even to quell thirst, since it was often contaminated. Only pure spring water could be trusted. The esteemed encyclopaedist Bartholomeus Anglicus declared in the thirteenth century that north-flowing spring water was of the highest quality, as the northerly winds made the water finer and lighter. In order of safety, spring water was followed by river water, lake water, pond water and marsh water, and there was always good reason to boil the latter four. According to medical experts, water was unsuitable to drink with food because of its cold and moist distinctive properties, which rendered it harmful to the digestion. Alcoholic drinks, on the other hand, were nourishing, clean and beneficial to the digestion.

Wine for the Wise

In France, Italy and Spain wine was the principal drink in the Middle Ages. Townspeople drank an average of one litre of wine per day, and peasants and labourers 1½ to 2 litres. There were numerous types of wines, both red and white. White wines were made either from white grapes or from dark grapes from which the skin had been removed, and could be consumed young, immediately following fermentation. Red wines involved the skins as well, and the vinification lasted longer. Wines differed considerably in quality and price: only wealthy laypeople and high-ranking members of the clergy could afford the finest and most expensive red wines. The alcohol content of inferior and cheaper wines such as whites and rosés was low, around 5 per cent by volume. Most people drank these, usually diluted with water, thus creating a thirst-quenching drink that could be consumed throughout the day without causing drunkenness.

Social, economic, agricultural and regional circumstances affected both the quality and the price of wine. Grapes were cultivated fairly effortlessly in the benign climatic conditions of the South, and wine could be exported at relatively low cost. The international wine trade flourished, and there was a large selection of vintages available for those who had the means to pay. The Flemish were ardent importers of wine from western France to the Low Countries and northern German states, while the English wine trade was concentrated on the merchant

127

harbours of France and the Hanseatic League. The province of Gascony in southwest France was held by England between 1152 and 1453, producing enough good-quality wine to meet national needs at home. In the North the climate did not encourage the growing of grapes, and wines were therefore imported from other parts of Europe. Spanish wines were popular, being strong and full-bodied. They were thought to cure a number of complaints, for example, galvanizing the internal organs, drying out infected wounds and fortifying the lungs. In the wine bars of Nordic cities French and German wines were readily available at reasonable cost.

Sweet, spiced wines were popular in the late Middle Ages, although they were not enjoyed at mealtimes together with food, but as aperitifs or digestifs, and usually in rather small measures. The best-known medieval spiced wine is hippocras,

77 Wine-drinking in the Nordic countries in a woodcut from Olaus Magnus's work. People of the North certainly enjoyed their wine. In his prayer book Mikael Agricola describes the month of October as the time when wine berries – grapes – are ready to be picked, and winter lurks around the corner. Leaves are falling from branches of trees, and in the butcher's shop, the rod strikes its victim in the forehead. Folk are encouraged to bathe, cup and bleed themselves, but to engage in nothing that involves the region below the belt. They should drink young wine, as it cleanses the body, and also take goat and sheep milk. Pepper and cloves could be added to the drink. Agricola used the Finnish word for hard liquor (*viina*) instead of wine, although he was not referring to strong, distilled alcohol. Goat's and sheep's milk were ingested for health reasons, and pepper and cloves were popular spices in many medieval drinks.

which got its name from Hippocrates (*c.* 460–*c.* 370 BC), the Greek physician regarded as the father of medicine. Numerous medieval recipe collections and manuscripts on gastronomy included instructions on how to make hippocras. The ingredients varied – the recipes reflecting economic changes and the individual and regional taste preferences at different times – but the key component was usually red wine blended with sugar and ground spices, normally ginger, cinnamon and pepper, and occasionally also nutmeg and cloves. Spice merchants carried ready-made hippocras mixes to be added directly to the wine, liberating busy or lazy housekeepers from the inconvenience of mixing spices in the midst of preparing supper.

From Barley to Beer

In England, the Netherlands, Germany and the Nordic countries beer was taken regularly with food. Hippocrates himself had spoken most highly of this drink made from barley. In the sixteenth century Olaus Magnus described the Nordic way of brewing beer from malted barley. First, the steeped and germinated grains were dried, at which point they sweetened. They were then ground fairly coarsely at the mill and poured into hot water to swell and sweeten them further. The mush was strained into another receptacle, and hops were added to the liquid to achieve the desired sweetness or acerbity. A small amount of the dregs of old beer was also thrown in as 'leavening', and then the brew was left to ferment until ready. Barley beer was good for chest pains and anxieties. A beer-like drink could be brewed from wheat and oats as well, using the same

78 Inspecting and tasting a new vintage in a late medieval miniature. According to the learned, a good wine had warm and dry distinctive properties, and was therefore recommended to healthy adults as a mealtime drink. Taken in moderation, wine strengthened the joints, promoted good digestion, eliminated feelings of melancholy and pain, restored cheerfulness and good humour, and prevented ageing. Adding gold to the wine produced a potion that bolstered the heart. A nip of wine first thing in the morning could even get rid of a hangover – a cure that many still advocate today. Bad wine, on the other hand, had the opposite effect to good wine, and was harmful to a person's health. In his work *De sanitatis custodia* (1314), the Italian physician Giacomo Albini of the Piedmont region pointed out that no wine whatsoever was to be given to children under the age of five, and small measures only, diluted with water and uniquely at mealtimes, to children under fourteen. Erasmus of Rotterdam reaffirmed that both wine and beer damaged the well-being and temperament of the young. For that reason, and in the event that water was lacking, young people were best advised to drink small beer or wine diluted with water. Rotten teeth, bloated cheeks, impaired sight and lethargy – in other words, the untimely onset of old age – were, in later years, consequences of the dependency caused by undiluted wine.

79 A brewer at work in a medieval woodcut. In the wine regions of the South beer-drinking cultures were often held in contempt. The writings of the learned regarded beer and ale as superior to water, but inferior to wine. The author of the 13th-century *Regimen sanitatis Salernitanum*, or the *Salernian Rule of Health*, emphasized the importance of drinking beer in moderation, since the state of drunkenness it caused was worse than the ill effects of wine. At the beginning of a meal, however, it might be preferable to drink beer rather than wine. Aldobrandino of Siena, for his part, warned that beer damaged both the head and stomach, caused bad breath and ruined the teeth. On the other hand, it facilitated urinating, and whitened and softened the skin. The English physician and writer Andrewe Boorde (*c.* 1490–1549) explained the difference between ale and beer: ale was made from malt and water, and was the chosen drink of the English. Beer was made from malt, hops and water, and was the drink of the Dutch. Not until 1525 was the hop plant brought to England from Flanders, but it had been used in the Low Countries for hundreds of years. The Dutch town of Amersfoort counted some 350 beer breweries in the 14th century; Haarlem a mere 50. *Godale,* a popular drink in France, was a strong, beer-like brew made from barley and wheat, but without hops. Various spices could be added to ale; in England spiced ale was called braggot or brakott.

method. Rye was rarely used for beer, since it was reserved primarily for bread-making. Unlike elsewhere in Europe, beer-brewing in the Nordic countries was often a task that fell upon women, except at princely courts, aristocratic homes or great monasteries.

The processing of grains prior to brewing varied, as did the brewing process itself. Olaus Magnus was of the opinion that the Finns knew best how to make beer out of oats – a brew that bolstered the ability to endure hardship, and helped the drinker to carry out even the most difficult of tasks. This oaten beer did not send people into a state of fury as certain wines did, nor did it render women barren, but quite the opposite. Oat beer also cured oedema and kidney stones and many other ailments. In the same way that wines improved the further south one travelled, the more enjoyable beer became the closer one returned towards the North. The German nations were of course known for both their wines and their beers, both of which were exported to the Nordic countries as well. Already in 1000, the Abbey of St Gall owned three large beer breweries, each producing a different type of beer. The oldest known licence issued by the Church to operate a brewery was the 947 deed granted by Notker, Bishop of Liège. The continuing growth of breweries in German monasteries also manifested itself in various health problems suffered by the friars, such as oedema and bladder- and prostate-related complaints, none of which, however, were ascribed to beer.

80 These decorative drinking vessels (*kousa*) were elaborate tankards used in southwest Finland in the late Middle Ages. Large amounts of beer-based drinks were consumed in northern Europe, on weekdays and feast days alike. In Finland, too, beer was an important part of daily sustenance. Naantali Abbey operated its own brewery. In accordance with abbey rules, the best-quality beer was to be reserved for the brewery manager, the second-best for the monks and nuns, and the rest was for pilgrims to purchase. In Swedish monasteries the monks were allotted a daily ration of three litres of beer, while at Enköping Hospital patients were given two helpings of beer per day; on Wednesdays they had buttermilk, and on Saturdays milk. By order of Gustav Vasa, King of Sweden (1496–1560), the highest-ranking officers of the army were to have so-called 'nobleman's beer', the lower-ranking officers 'bailiff's beer', and everybody else 'squire's beer' or mild 'naval beer'. Nobleman's beer was roughly the strength of present-day, cask-conditioned ale. In the Nordic countries the hops needed for flavouring beer were bought from the merchants of the German Hanseatic League in the early Middle Ages. The 1442 Land Acts of King Christopher called for every peasant and tenant farmer to grow 40 hop plants. In 1474 the number was increased to 200, and non-compliance could bring penalties. The aim was to balance the nation's economy. According to the latest archaeological research, the cultivation of hops was widespread in Finland.

Cider, Mead and Spirits

In the Middle Ages fruit and berry juices were also often made good use of, whether fresh or fermented. Especially in northern regions, apple cider (German *Zider* or French *pommé*) was quite a common drink. According to the learned, apple cider particularly benefited those of a choleric disposition and those who worked outdoors. Apples had been cultivated for thousands of years – the oldest data are from *c.* 3000 BC – while apple-growing in the Nordic countries developed only in the high

medieval era, concurrently with the advance of Christianity, the Crusades and the growing number of monastic orchards. In Finland the actual cultivation of apples got under way in the fifteenth and sixteenth centuries. The first substantiated information on apple-growing comes from Kuitia Manor in Parainen, where State Councillor Erik Fleming established a fruit orchard in 1539. The apple saplings were acquired in neighbouring Tallinn.

Pear cider – or perry (French *poiré*) – was made as well, wherever pears grew and were appreciated. Various wine-like drinks were fermented from wild plums (*prunellé*), sloes or mulberries (murrey in England; *muré* in France), all of which were highly popular, especially in England and France. Pomegranate drinks and wines were fairly common in Italy. In the Nordic countries wine substitutes were produced not only from apples and pears, but from rowanberries and medlars. Pepper, ginger and cloves were used as seasoning. Other common plants used in drinks were sage, absinth wormwood, rue and lavender, all of which lent their names to their respective fruit drinks.

In Finland ordinary people usually drank buttermilk (*piimä*) or *kalja*, a type of small beer, at mealtimes. Both would be diluted with water. Mead, honey drinks, *kalja* and beer were often brewed for special occasions. Beer blended with mead or honeyed water was also a popular festive drink referred to as *mjölska* or *mölska* in Swedish texts. Mead went a long way back in history: since time immemorial honey had been dissolved in water, particularly in northern Europe and the Celtic communities. The Vikings believed mead to be endowed with

godly powers, conferring immortality and wisdom upon man. The Finnish word *sima*, meaning 'mead', was a Germanic loan which arrived in Finland by way of Scandinavia, initially linked to the word *mesi*, 'honey' or 'nectar'. Elsewhere mead was known as *medo* and *mellicrattum* (Latin), *mede* in England and Germany, and *bochet* in France. A late fourteenth-century English recipe for mead simply suggested boiling honey in water. In the Germanic nations mead was a more popular drink, and the brewing methods more complex. The late fourteenth-century instructions for mead in the French

household manual *Ménagier de Paris* also necessitated fermentation.

As regards strong, distilled alcoholic drinks or spirits (*aqua vitae*), these were not consumed in any noteworthy quantities in the Middle Ages, particularly not at mealtimes. That said, small amounts of strong alcohol could be added to spiced wine and ale. Medieval chefs also used alcohol to carry off various special effects involving fire, such as conjuring up fire-breathing dragons or peacocks for entremets during courtly palace suppers.

Only small amounts of alcohol were distilled, and, up until the end of the Middle Ages, mainly

82 The Devil's bacchanal in full swing in the tavern. Moralists and conservatives repeteadly condemned heavy drinking in the Middle Ages.

in the monasteries. The sale of *aqua vitae* and refined alcohol products was concentrated in cities and pharmacies. In thirteenth- and fourteenth-century Nuremberg, for instance, apothecaries might have carried different brands such as *gebrannter Wein*, *Bernewein* and *Brandwein*. As for the price, spirits were within the reach of ordinary folk as well, and as time went by the use of strong alcohol gradually became anchored in everyday custom.

The German Dominican friar Albert the Great (1193–1280) suggested two methods for distilling firewater, or *aqua ardens*. Medical experts appreciated the refined and light composition of strong alcohol. Also it was said to cure many ills. The alchemist, astrologer and physician Arnaldus de Villa Nova (1235–1311) wrote in 1309 that 'water of life' promoted longevity and good health, since it destroyed excess bodily fluids, stimulated the heart and sustained a person's youthfulness. Spirits also cured oedema, colic, paralysis, fevers and chills, and gallstones.

Taverns: Temples of Evil

Although alcoholic beverages were mild in the Middle Ages, people succumbed to intoxication all the same, be they high-born or low, lay or members of the clergy. Court records show that alcohol played a significant part in the majority of violent crimes committed in the late Middle Ages. Drunken sprees, particularly in public houses, often ended in violent skirmishes and manslaughter. Not without reason did moralists refer to taverns as 'the Devil's temples'. A decent Christian could only hope to escape ruin by making a wide detour around such nests of sin.

Large cities were home to a vast number of public houses in the late Middle Ages. In the Flemish town of Ypres the authorities tried to limit their number to one for every eight households. Paris counted over 4,000 wine bars selling 700 barrels of wine every day, each barrel holding approximately 120 litres. The taverns were located near the city gates in the busy parts of town. In his work the poet François Villon mentioned several Parisian taverns by their names: The Great Fig Tree, The Pine Cone, The Helm, The White Horse, The Mule, The Great Chalice, The Wine Barrel and so on. The taverns were not only frequented for drinking, but for gambling purposes as well. Not all public houses served food, although salted herring was often available to purchase, an item that naturally increased the thirst of the patrons.

In the Nordic countries inns and taverns took care of travellers, offering room and board and feed for the horses. Merchants and craftsmen gathered in the public rooms to eat and drink, discuss professional matters, gamble, sing and play music.

Medieval preachers fought valiantly against this deplorable sin of drunkenness. Moralists, too, drew stern attention to the need for a good Christian and decent, civilized human being to observe moderation in drink. Food and drink were to be treated as medicine, working towards the welfare of the individual rather than any hedonistic pleasures. The English poet Geoffrey Chaucer (c. 1343–1400) pointed out that excess drinking and drunkenness led to loss of memory and good judgement, and that the drunkard easily succumbed to other sins and misdemeanours.

Many medieval chroniclers, who considered educational goals to be of utmost importance, recounted cautionary tales of the dangers posed by intoxication. Exemplary sobriety was most commonly advocated in the life stories of the saints, among them the French chronicler Jean de Joinville's (1225–1317) famous work on Louis IX of France, also known as St Louis. Similarly the piousness of Joan of Arc (d. 1431) was highlighted by calling attention to the fact that the maiden always diluted her wine with water, and never drank more than one small goblet at a time.

In the sixteenth century the Swedish historian Olaus Magnus called to mind that, in the words of the Greek philosopher Plato, the drunkard becomes a child for a second time, and that drunkenness was a punishable offence even when it did not result in manslaughter. Intoxicating oneself was a senseless pursuit. Excessive wine drinking made the French lewd, the Germans quarrelsome, the Geats (a north Germanic tribe inhabiting parts of Sweden) rebellious and the Finns tearful – in fact, every drunkard seemed afflicted by every one of these traits. Olaus Magnus speculated that an appropriate punishment for a drunkard might be to place him on a wedge-shaped seat that could be hoisted aloft with the help of ropes. The drunkard would be given a full beaker of beer, and could then choose between emptying the beaker promptly or remaining seated on the sharp stool and experiencing the consequences of craving drink.

The authors of medieval conduct books attached great importance to decent drinking habits during mealtimes. On festive occasions, too, restraint had to be observed with regard to the drinks consumed with food. Beginning a meal with a shot of hard liquor revealed a drunkard who did not drink for want of fluid, but to indulge a habit — conduct that was not only morally degrading, but harmful to the health as well. Nor was one to start drinking immediately after having tasted the first spoonful of soup. Having more than a couple of glassfuls during the course of a banquet was thought unseemly, if not directly unhealthy, particularly for the young. The first serving should not be taken until the second course, and the second serving

not until the end of the feast. Moreover, the drink was to be enjoyed in modest sips rather than being downed immediately, which made the diner 'sound like a horse swallowing', as Erasmus of Rotterdam put it.

You were supposed to chew your food before taking a swallow from your glass, and you were not to lift your glass to your lips until you had wiped your mouth clean on a napkin, particularly not if someone offered you his goblet, or if you drank out of a communal glass. 'By the same token, you must attentively acknowledge anybody raising his glass to you. Grasp your own glass, touch it briefly to your lips and let it be known that you, too, have drunk: this is enough to satisfy a courteous gentleman', Erasmus counselled.

When drinking together, people should be allowed to speak freely. Afterwards it was dishonourable to bring to light anything that anybody else may mistakenly have let slip during dinner. What was said or done could be ascribed to the wine, so that no one later felt compelled to say that they abhorred drinking in the company of those who remembered everything. ⊲

Er parle dune grant feste que le roy richard dengleterre fist a londres

83 Richard II dines with the Dukes of York, Gloucester and Ireland. The most famous English recipe collection, the *Forme of Cury*, was created by Richard's chefs.

ten

IN SEARCH OF A FORGOTTEN WORLD OF FLAVOURS

Researching medieval food culture is a fascinating but challenging task. Tracing a world of flavours from the past may seem ambitious – naturally pork tasted like pork and ginger like ginger even 600 years ago, but what did the finished dish made from these and other ingredients truly taste like? Attempting to find an answer can be daunting when the exact quantities, proportions and procedures remain obscure, on account of the fact that the recipes of the time are annoyingly uncommunicative about details. Chroniclers of music focusing on the Middle Ages, for instance, find themselves confronted by a similar dilemma: on the basis of old musical notations and the few instruments that still exist, along with illustrations in contemporary writings, it is extremely difficult to divine what fourteenth- to fifteenth-century music truly sounded like. Further complications arise from the fact that medieval perceptions and sensations, such as feelings of enjoyment or aversion, are sentiments of the past and therefore subject to evaluation according to time and place. What is perceived as pleasant and harmonious today may have come across as quite the opposite to those who lived in bygone times.

A Cornucopia of Texts

When exploring the forgotten world of flavours, texts, archaeological evidence and picture references become essential primary sources for historians researching medieval food. As previously mentioned, the written source material includes not only cookery books and recipe collections, but also bills of fare, tax records, ledgers, wills and testaments, diaries, chronicles and encyclopaedias, as well as housekeeping, health, etiquette, hunting and cattle-raising manuals, and even fictional texts ranging from tales of knights in shining armour to fairy tales and poems. Plays, drinking songs, allegories and proverbs might also be of use.

Cookery books, recipe collections and bills of fare inform us first and foremost about the customs, preferences and ideals of the upper classes. Peacocks, cranes and swans were certainly not everyone's fare, nor did everybody flavour their food with saffron, ginger and sugar. Since medieval cookery books often lack measurements and cooking instructions, food historians are compelled to carry out scores of trial performances when trying to delve into and get acquainted with the flavours of the past in practice. And

MEDIEVAL COOKERY BOOKS AND RECIPE COLLECTIONS

The kitchen of ancient Rome was made famous through the much-copied recipe collection of the epicure Marcus Gavius Apicius, who lived in the first century during the reigns of Augustus and Tiberius. After Apicius a long lull ensued, and the next recipe collections date from as recently as the early fourteenth century. Approximately one hundred fourteenth- and fifteenth-century collections are left with us today. These are not independent efforts, since the authors copied recipes from one another and from communal sources.

In epicurism, differences were greater between the social classes than between the nations, and numerous recipes reappear in cookery books from different parts of Europe. Although much is being repeated, the ingredients and cooking techniques still vary to some degree, and it is precisely these slight variations that make the researcher's work so interesting.

The first European cookery books were general works. Speciality treatises on epicurism did not appear until the mid-sixteenth century, and these included, alongside recipes for upper-class feasts, instructions for everyday cooking. Most of the medieval collections that are left today were re-edited and publicized in the twentieth century, with the exception of certain German compendia, of which some are yet to be researched. Of the German recipe collections, the best known are the fourteenth-century *Buch von guter Speize*, which reflects the taste preferences of the Bishop of Würzburg, the *Kochbuch Meister Eberhards*, written by the head chef at the Bavarian court in the early fifteenth century, and the *Küchenmaistrey* from *c.* 1495.

Worth mentioning among the Italian collections are the fourteenth-century *Tractatus de modo preparandi et condiendi ominia cibaria*, which bears close comparison with the writings that approach food from a medical point of view, the Neapolitan *Liber de coquina*, and the hands-on, anonymous, late fourteenth-century *Il libro della cocina* and *Il libro per cuoco*, issuing out of Tuscany and Venice respectively. A noteworthy fifteenth-century publication is Jean de Bockenheim's Latin-language cookery book *Registrum coquine* (*c.* 1430). The author served as head chef to Pope Martin V, and the book's approach to food is multidimensional in that it makes a distinction between the various dishes favoured by different social groups and nationalities. Among the most well-known Italian works is the mid-fifteenth-century treatise *Libro de arte coquinaria* by Maestro Martino, who served as chef at the household of the Patriarch of Aquileia. This text was possibly aimed at a wider audience, as it contained more uncomplicated instructions than those of its predecessors. Notwithstanding, Maestro Martino was in his own time little known outside his country's borders, despite working within the highest churchly circles. The humanist and writer Bartolomeo Sacchi (1421–1481), better known under the name Battista Platina, Prefect of the Vatican Library, published 240 of Maestro Martino's 250 recipes in Latin in his work *De honesta voluptate et valetudine* in 1475. The newfound use of the printing press enabled translated copies of the book to spread to different parts of Europe. In his work Platina merges the theory behind Martino's cooking expertise with moral and social themes.

Well known among the English texts are the fourteenth-century *Diuersa Cibaria*, with didactic undertones, and the more comprehensive *Diuersa Servisa*. However, the most famous of all is the *Forme of Cury* from around 1390, created by the head chefs of Richard II (1377–1399) in collaboration with medical experts. Several fifteenth-century collections still remain today, among them the *Utilis Coquinario* and *Liber Cure Cocorum*, as well as the *Kalendare de Potages, Leche Metys, Dyuerse Bakematis* (*c.* 1430), *A Boke of Kokery* (*c.* 1450) and *A Noble Boke off Cookryn* (*c.* 1460). Many fifteenth-century English cookery books are sourced from non-royal households, and so provide concise accounts of the heritage left by the previous century.

From the French region, a number of anonymous texts have been preserved, some of them bearing the name of a master chef. The most famous of the texts circulated under the title *Le Viandier* was composed already in the early fourteenth century, but was later linked to Guillaume Tirel, head chef at the courts of Charles V and Charles VI of France. The recipe section in the work *Ménagier de Paris* (1392–4) can also be counted among the most famous French collections. The first part of the book deals with the expected behaviour and obligations of a Christian wife; the second with being the mistress of a house and running a household; and the third with leisure activities. The work was written by a wealthy Parisian burgher or civil servant of a certain age as a guideline to his newlywed, fifteen-year-old wife, and includes many favourite recipes of the era. Of the 380 cooking instructions, some 85 are taken from the *Viandier* collection. The directions are more specific than was the norm, and come equipped with critical observations, targeting a readership that is not made up of professional chefs but novices in the field. Still to be mentioned among the works from France are the *Grand cuisinier de toute cuisine* and *Du fait de cuisine*, of which the latter was concluded in 1420, supplementing the two aforementioned. It was created by Maître Chiquart, head chef to Amadeus VIII, Duke of Savoy, and offers more precise explanations of, for instance, cooking techniques than its contemporaries.

Medieval cookery books were predominantly written by men. At the time written communication was gendered, and high-quality cooking was likewise deemed a male profession. Recipes were not compiled into books for the use of professional chefs, but as a result of their activities. The books may have served as an ancillary memory to literate head chefs, or as archive material documenting the procedures and practical expertise pertaining to important households. In the Middle Ages cookery was a discipline reserved for professionals, requiring a broad spectrum of skills: a master chef had to recognize and know by heart the appropriate quantities of the different ingredients involved, the cooking methods and techniques, the procedures, final goals, flavours and finished looks.

The relatively small number of cookery books and the inexactitude of the recipes can be ascribed to the prevailing tradition of oral communication. Information was handed down orally from master to apprentice, from mother to daughter. Illiteracy combined with the fact that the Church condemned anything linked to gluttony worked to the disadvantage of the evolution of culinary literature. For a long time cooking instructions were passed on verbally, and writing them down did not seem worthwhile. When medical science, striving for a higher scientific status, in due course began to focus on the pros and cons of food, the interest in cooking sprang to life and the compiling of culinary instructions became the speciality of professionals — that is to say, palace chefs.

A key factor in the growing number of cookery books in the fourteenth and fifteenth centuries is thought to have been the changing society, a phenomenon that first became apparent in the Italian city states. The rising new orders, first and foremost the bourgeoisie, yearned for cooking directives to bolster their struggle for upper-class refinement as they sought to assert their position in society. Nevertheless, in becoming more widespread, gastronomic publications also worked within increasingly wider circles in promoting the skills required for preparing both everyday and gourmet foods. So from this point of view the cookery books had a popularizing impact. The progress was also linked to the general expansion of literature in the late Middle Ages. Although cookery books were predominantly written in the vernacular — in other words, they were comprehensible to those who did not have Latin — in practice they were intended primarily for those who could afford the realization of the recipes: the upper crust.

87 A marriage feast, in an early 15th-century illustration from John of Berry's book of hours. The table is laid with round loaves of bread, meat and wine.

Festive Menu Suggestions for a
Medieval-style Supper

Light Springtime Supper

Sage wine as a welcome drink (p. 210)
Vegetable and herb pie (p. 158)
Baked pike with white wine sauce (p. 176), spelt frumenty (p. 151)
Spiced pear soup (p. 199), pine nut fondants (p. 207)

Romantic Summer Supper

Stuffed button mushrooms (p. 161)
Chicken in red wine sauce (p 165), savoury barley pudding (p. 150)
Rose pudding (p. 204)

Tasty Autumn Supper

Honey-glazed turnips (p. 155)
English lamb stew (p. 162), spelt frumenty (p. 151)
Layered almond milk pudding (p. 200), orange wine (p. 211)

Hearty Winter Supper

Carrot and caraway soup (p. 154)
Parisian hare stew (p. 171), rice accompaniment (p. 152),
Tuscan wild mushrooms (p. 159), and berry jelly (for instance, rowanberry jelly)
Walnut and date pie (p. 205), almond cream (p. 202)
Hippocras (p. 208), postprandial parlour spices (p. 189)

88 Demons and diners with different types and shapes of breads from a mural painting in St Lawrence, Lohja, Finland. Account books from the royal castles of Häme and Turku in Finland in the 16th century list rye, barley and sourdough bread in addition to *rievä* – fresh, soft barley bread – and the wheaten loaves and rolls intended for the royal table. At Turku Castle in 1546, herrainleipä or 'nobleman's bread' – soft, luxurious bread made from refined flour – graced the bailiff's table, while the workers had bran bread. At the table of Duke John in 1563, wheaten loaves and rolls and bread made from other refined flours featured prominently – but no bran bread. Wheat bread was an upper-class delicacy in the Nordic countries, whereas further south in Europe, it was accessible to the common people as well, although on a somewhat smaller scale than the cheaper, darker bread types. In southwest Finland, from the late Middle Ages onwards, dark bread was sweetened with malt and rye.

Medieval Recipes for Modern Cooks

Grain products

Nettle Bread

600 ml (1¼ pints) lukewarm water
180 g (2½ cups) shredded fresh nettle leaves
1–2 tsp salt
2 tsp caraway seeds
50 g (1¾ oz) yeast
170 g (1⅔ cups) coarse-ground rye flour
500–650 g (4¼ – 5½ cups) dark wheat flour

Stir the salt, yeast, caraway seeds and nettles into the lukewarm water. Add both types of flour and knead thoroughly. Leave the dough to rise until it doubles in size. Knead it again, and mould the dough into round loaves. Leave the loaves to rise further on a baking sheet, and bake for 40–50 minutes in a 175–200°C (350–390°F) oven.

Apart from being used as nourishment, the nettle was also a common medicinal herb in the Middle Ages. If you wish, you can pierce a small hole in the loaf before baking. This medieval custom arrived in Finland from south-west Sweden. The hole was located on the side of the loaf and threaded with string, by which the bread could be suspended from a bread pole to dry.

I have developed this recipe with reference to Ulla Lehtonen's *Luonnon hyötykasvien keruu- ja käyttöopas* and Anna-Liisa Neuvonen.

Unleavened Barley Bread

250 ml (8½ fl. oz) warm water
1 tsp salt
1 tbsp oil
approx. 200 g (2 cups) barley flour

Stir the salt into the warm water and add the oil and flour. Mix the dough evenly. Sprinkle a baking board generously with barley flour. Work the dough into a roll and cut it into slices. Mould each slice into a round, flat cake approximately 0.5 cm thick. Place the cakes onto a baking sheet lined with baking parchment, and prick them with a fork. Bake for 10–12 minutes in a 250°C (480°F) oven. Serve hot with butter. If you prefer crisper cakes, make them thinner and bake them a little longer. This recipe is from the folk tradition of central Finland; the source was Anna-Liisa Neuvonen.

Jo otti ohraleipä is an old Finnish saying denouncing barley bread as unwholesome and inferior. Unleavened barley bread is the oldest type of bread in the Nordic countries. Hugely popular in the Middle Ages, the second-century bestiary *Physiologus*, a study on the actual and mythological characteristics of animals and the moral or religious symbolism they epitomized, praised the exemplary industriousness and wisdom of ants, using barley as a negative example. The ants recognized barley and rye – seen as cattle fodder – by their smell, and so collected only wheat. A good Christian, too, was to avoid animal feed and consume grain that stood the test of time, such as wheat. 'Barley is like the teachings of heretics, while wheat equates to true Christian faith.' The lead-up to this allegory were the parables of Jesus illustrating the sower and the crop, and the wheat and the tares (Matthew 13:1–13, 18–30). However, the Italian writer Bartolomeo Platina (1421–1481), author of the *De honesta voluptate et valetudine* ('On honourable pleasure and health'), maintained that barley bread was also 'of a most noble sort', although wheat bread was still without equal.

Saffron Bread

approx. 1 kg (8½ cups) medium-ground wheat flour
500 ml (1 pint) warm water
35 g (1¼ oz) yeast
175 g (¾ cup) sugar
1½–2 tsp salt
100 ml (½ cup) olive oil
3 eggs
pinch of saffron

Stir the yeast into the warm water. Add the seasoning, oil, eggs and flour. Knead. Cover the dough with a cloth and leave it to rise. Form five medium-sized, round loaves, and leave them to rise further on a baking sheet. Bake on the lower rack in a 200°C (390°F) oven for approximately 15 minutes or until the crust is beautifully brown. You can carve the shape of a cross onto the surface of each loaf during the second rising stage. A medieval tradition was to bless the batch with the sign of the cross, and to draw a cross onto the first fruits of the dough.

I have developed this recipe, as well as the one below, with reference to Josy Marty-Dufaut's *La Gastronomie du Moyen Age*.

Ginger Loaves

500 g (4 cups) medium-coarse wheat flour
170 g (1 cup) semolina
500 ml (1 pint) warm water
35–50 g (1¼–1½ oz) yeast
1 tbsp salt
3–4 tsp ground ginger
1 tsp ground cinnamon

Dissolve the yeast and seasoning in the warm water. Add the flour and semolina. Knead. Cover the dough with a cloth and leave it to rise for an hour or until the dough has doubled in size. Form two or three loaves, and leave them to rise further on a baking sheet. Prick the loaves with a fork and bake for approximately 30 minutes on the lower rack of a 200°C (390°F) oven.

89 Two bakers at work in a large bakehouse. A wealth of symbolism involving bread comes to light in numerous old sayings: bread is the staff of life; all sorrows are less with bread; bread never falls but on its buttered side; to butter one's bread on both sides; to cast one's bread upon the waters – the list is endless.

Savoury Barley Pudding

90 g (½ cup) wholegrain barley

500 ml (1 pint) water

500 ml (1 pint) vegetable stock

4 radishes

2 carrots

oil

2 tbsp chopped cress

½ tsp ground black pepper

½ tsp ground cinnamon

½ tsp salt

Soak the barley in water overnight. (Pre-cooked barley, too, is best soaked for an hour or so.) Strain and place in a saucepan. Add the vegetable stock and bring to a boil. Let simmer over a moderate heat for approximately 35 minutes. Strain the cooking liquid and rinse the barley in a sieve. Cut the carrots and radishes into short, thin strips and sauté them in oil in the saucepan until soft. Add the chopped cress, seasoning and barley. Taste and reheat the pudding, stirring over a moderate heat. Serve, for instance, as an accompaniment to meat.

The radish in this recipe is one of the very oldest cultivated vegetables, although it did not arrive in Europe from China until the sixteenth century. Its pungent flavour comes from a mustard oil present in radishes, and is similar to that of the mooli or icicle radish, an even older type of *Raphanus sativus*. Both species are related to the field radish. Radishes come in many colours, although the oldest varieties are white. The various cress plants, on the other hand, are leaf vegetables related to cabbage and mustard, cultivated since ancient times in Europe and the Middle East. Watercress, for one, is rich in beneficial trace minerals and vitamins. Due to its slightly bitter taste, it has not been used routinely in large quantities in food preparation.

The sources for this recipe were Mary Savelli, The Oulu Medieval Association and the author.

Spelt Frumenty

260 g (1½ cups) pearlized spelt
800 ml (1¾ pints) vegetable, chicken or beef stock
2 egg yolks
pinch of saffron or ginger

Bring the stock to a boil in a saucepan and add the spelt. Cover and let simmer until the liquid is absorbed, or approximately 20 minutes. Remove from heat. Add the saffron and whisked egg yolks. Gently reheat until the mixture thickens. Serve as an accompaniment to meat. Although more common in the South, spelt is found to have been cultivated in the North as well in the fifteenth century.

A late fourteenth-century recipe for frumenty from the *Forme of Cury* collection of recipes compiled by the chefs of King Richard II of England reads as follows:

> *To make frumente. Tak clene whete & braye yt wel in a morter tyl Þe holes gon of; sepe it til it breste in water. Nym it vp & lat it cole. Tak good broÞ & swete mylk of kyn or of almand & tempere it Þerewith. Nym yelkys of eyren rawe & saffroun & cast Þerto; salt it; lat it nauyt boyle after Þe eyren ben cast Þerinne. Messe it forth with venesoun or with fat motoun fresch.*

In other words, the ingredients listed are crushed wheat, beef stock or milk or alternatively almond milk, egg yolks, saffron and salt. The wheat is boiled in water until the grains split. The cooking liquid is discarded and the grains are rinsed, dried and set aside to cool. Beef stock or milk is placed into a saucepan, along with the cooked wheat. The mixture is brought to a boil and left to simmer over a moderate heat, occasionally stirred. Last, the whisked egg yolks and seasoning are added, and the lot is left to simmer for a further several minutes, avoiding boiling. Frumenty is well suited to game or mutton. A late fourteenth-century French recipe from the *Ménagier de Paris* suggests a pinch of ginger instead of saffron.

Rice Accompaniment for Meat

160 g (¾ cup) rice
500 ml (1 pint) chicken or beef stock
½ portion almond milk (recipe on p. 186)
pinch of saffron
salt

Place the chicken or beef stock and rice in a saucepan, bring to a boil and let it simmer over low heat. In a separate saucepan, prepare half a portion of almond milk. When ready, add the almond milk to the rice. Let the concoction simmer for a further 10 minutes or until the rice is cooked. Taste and add salt, if needed. Serve together with meat. I have taken this *Ryse of Flessh* recipe from the *Forme of Cury* collection, with reference to *Medieval Cooking Today* by Moira Buxton.

Parisian Porridge

175 g (1 cup) pre-cooked wholegrain barley
400 ml (12 fl. oz) water
2 litres (4 pints) almond milk (recipe on p. 186)
2 tsp salt
generous amounts of sugar

Add the barley to the boiling water and let boil until the water is absorbed. Add the almond milk and let simmer over a moderate heat for approximately 1 hour, stirring occasionally. Season with salt and sugar,

90 In Gerard David's painting, the porridge has a milk base as a reference to Mary's purity and her role as a mother. The bread beside the apple, the symbol of Original Sin, was a symbol of redemption in medieval religious iconography.

and serve. I have developed this porridge from the *Ménagier de Paris* (1392–4). You can give the porridge further sparkle by adding eggs, cardamom, cinnamon and a pinch of ground nutmeg.

Porridge recipes are relatively rare in medieval cookery books, since porridge-making belonged to every cook's basic skills. Moreover porridge was often associated with the poor or the infirm. For the sickly, sugar was added to the porridge not only for taste but also for health reasons.

Vegetables

Carrot and Caraway Soup

1 kg (2 lb) carrots
2 litres (4 pints) water
2–3 vegetable bouillon cubes
1 tbsp caraway seeds
100 ml (½ cup) cream

Peel and cut the carrots, and boil until soft. Reserve the cooking liquid; purée the carrots separately. Add the bouillon cubes and the puréed carrots to the cooking liquid, bring to a boil and add the caraway seeds and cream. This is a mild, good-tasting soup that works well as a starter together with white bread.

Carrots were cultivated in Spain and Asia Minor already in the twelfth century. They were used as both food and medicine, and also as a colourant. In the late Middle Ages carrots could also be found in various vegetable compotes for the upper classes. In the Nordic countries the carrot long remained a rarity reserved for vicarages and manor houses. The orange-coloured carrot known to us was developed in Holland in the eighteenth century – prior to that, carrots were purplish-red, yellow or white. Today small amounts of yellow or red carrots are being cultivated once more.

I have developed this recipe with reference to Josy Marty-Dufaut's *La Gastronomie du Moyen Age*.

Stewed Leeks

4–6 leeks (preferably young)
2 onions
oil
300–400 ml (10–14 fl. oz) almond milk (recipe on p. 186)
approx. 1 tsp salt
½ tsp black pepper

Use only the pale parts of the leeks. In a saucepan, sauté the chopped leeks and onions in oil until soft; do not brown. Prepare the almond

91 A peasant picking leeks, in a medieval woodcut.

milk, add to the leek and onion mixture and let simmer for approximately 20 minutes, stirring occasionally. Finally, purée briefly in a blender and season to taste.

The leek was a particularly popular vegetable related to the onion, its pale cylindrical bulb the favoured part. In France *la porée* (from the Latin *porrum*) was a typical soup between the twelfth and sixteenth centuries, made from leeks or other vegetables. This *porée blanche* recipe is originally from the *Ménagier de Paris*, an anonymous household manual written in late fourteenth-century France. During days of fasting, almond milk was used as cooking liquid; on meat-eating days, the stew was prepared with cow's milk and lard. The stew works well as a starter or as an accompaniment to ham or pork.

Honey-glazed Turnips

turnips
beef stock
butter or oil
spices or honey

Slice the turnips into approximately 1–1½ cm thick slices. Cook the pieces in beef stock until soft but still firm. Add butter or oil to a frying pan and brown the slices to a pretty colour. Sprinkle with spices or coat with generous amount of honey. If you wish, you can replace the turnips with swedes, which have a milder flavour.

Hearth and Home

The hearth was the centre of culinary activity in medieval housekeeping. In ordinary homes people seated themselves around the hearth to dine, whether with other members of the family or with guests. Since boiling and frying took place over an open flame, regulating the fire was a demanding task. Pots and pans had to be kept far enough from the flames, an effort facilitated by legs or tripods supporting the cookware alongside adjustable pothooks, slots and chains. Another pitfall involving cooking on an open fire was the risk of the food tasting of smoke, as chimneys were not yet common. Flues leading outdoors did exist, although they were not always adequate conduits for the smoke.

Wood was used as fuel, but since it was difficult to adjust the flames in order to maintain an even temperature, kitchens of a more substantial size switched from wood to coal in the fifteenth century. Considerable amounts of both wood and coal were needed for food preparation. Private homes were rarely equipped with ovens, although communal ovens were readily available in town and countryside alike. These were intended primarily for bread baking, since pies and tarts could be baked at home in receptacles placed in the grate. There was little or no ovenware suitable for baking, as clay cracked easily in high temperatures, and iron heated up too slowly and copper too fast — hence the great popularity of baking food inside a pie shell.⌐

92 A peasant dining in front of the hearth, in a medieval calendar.

This recipe originates in late fourteenth-century France. The turnip was a popular root vegetable in medieval Europe, since it soaked up grease and went well with various spices. Turnips were already established in Finland before the year I BC at a time when slash and burn agriculture was being implemented. Throughout the Middle Ages up until the nineteenth century, the turnip was part of the daily fare of common people. In remote areas, as the use of fire to clear land was discontinued, the turnip was eventually replaced by the potato, which arrived in Finland in the eighteenth century. The mature turnip has a very particular flavour, simultaneously sweet and aromatic, and not too bitter.

Turnip and Parsnip Soup

300 g (2 cups) turnips cut into chunks
190 g (1¼ cups) parsnips cut into chunks
1 litre (2 pints) vegetable stock
115 g (1 cup) coarse-ground almonds
500 ml (1 pint) cream
6 egg yolks
½ tsp salt
juice of ½ lemon

In the Middle Ages turnip soup was considered an excellent remedy for coughs. The cultivation of parsnips had begun in ancient Greece and Rome, but did not spread to northern Europe until the Middle Ages. Like the carrot, the parsnip first emerged on the scene among the upper classes. It was a well-liked vegetable, and was eaten either steamed or made into purées or soups.

I have developed this recipe with reference to Madeleine Pelner Cosman.

Mashed Swede

swede, water, salt, milk
butter, honey, dill

Peel and cut the swedes into chunks. Boil in salted water until soft. Drain the water and mash the swedes. Add milk and butter and heat to the point of boiling. Add the honey and chopped dill, which will give the mash an appealing hint of anise. Instead of dill, you can also use anise, and turnips instead of swedes, in which case you need to add more honey, as the flavour of turnips can be rather bitter. Mashed turnips with dill were often served with fish in the Middle Ages.

The swede is a cross between a turnip and a cabbage and was known from the sixteenth century onwards, when it was cultivated in the Nordic countries. Yet in Finnish agriculture, the turnip was a more important root vegetable than the swede.

Dill and caraway were the most common aromatic herbs in the Baltic region in the Middle Ages. Sixteenth-century ledgers from Häme and Turku Castles mention garden herbs such as thyme, rosemary, radish, horseradish, lavender, fennel, mint, clove and parsley.

I have developed this recipe with reference to Josy Marty-Dufaut's *La Gastronomie du Moyen Age*.

Vegetable and Herb Pie

crust:
125 g butter
350 ml (1½ cups) medium-coarse wheat flour
½ tsp salt
4 tbsp water

filling:
125 g (1½ cups) chopped chard
55 g (¾ cup) chopped fresh parsley
100 ml (½ cup) chopped fresh chervil
1 fennel stalk
55 g (¾ cup) chopped spinach
oil for cooking
100 g (3½ oz) cream cheese
grated cheese
3 eggs
½ tsp ground ginger or pepper
salt

Rinse and chop the vegetables and fresh herbs. Pan fry in oil until soft; season. Prepare the crust: with your fingertips, work wheat flour, salt and butter into a crumbly paste and incorporate water, working fast. Press the dough onto the bottom and sides of a baking pan with removable bottom (22 cm or 9 inches in diameter). Line the dough with greased kitchen foil, not forgetting the sides, and fill with dried peas. Blind-bake for 9 minutes on the middle shelf of a 200°C (390°F) oven. Remove peas and foil, prick the bottom of the crust all over with a fork and bake for a further 2–3 minutes. Spread the vegetable filling onto the piecrust. In a bowl, beat the eggs, add cream cheese and grated cheese and pour the mixture onto the vegetable filling. Bake in a 200°C (390°F) oven for 30–40 minutes or until the filling has solidified and taken on a bit of colour.

The source for this recipe is the *Ménagier de Paris*.

Tuscan Wild Mushrooms

600 g (1 lb 5 oz) forest mushrooms

2 onions

olive oil

1 tsp ground black pepper

1 tsp ground ginger

½ tsp ground nutmeg

2 tsp ground coriander

salt

In a pan, sauté the chopped mushrooms until the liquid from them has evaporated. Reserve. Gently sauté the chopped onions in oil, add the mushrooms and fry for a while. Season with the spices, cover and let simmer gently for approximately 15 minutes. Serve as an accompaniment to meat.

You can replace part of the forest mushrooms with cultivated button mushrooms, which cost less. This recipe appeared originally in the fourteenth-century Italian cookbook *Libro della cucina del secolo XIV*, and was developed by Odile Redon, Françoise Sabban and Silvano Serventi.

93 A master herbalist supervises the collecting of plants in a medieval manuscript illumination.

Stuffed Button Mushrooms

12–14 large button mushrooms

200 g (7 oz) plain cream cheese

1 large clove of garlic

1–2 slices white bread

1 tsp ground rosemary

1 tsp ground basil

1 tsp ground oregano

½ tsp salt

Rinse the mushrooms and remove the caps from the stems. Add the seasoning to the cream cheese. Toast and dice the bread and combine with the cheese. Stuff the mushroom caps with the mixture and replace the stems. Bake in a 180°C (355°F) oven for approximately 30 minutes until cooked. Serve warm or chilled.

From ancient times mushrooms were known both as food and as potentially poisonous. In medieval thinking mushrooms were associated with the temptation to evil and the wordly pleasures that led men away from the spiritual path.

The button mushroom grows in the wild in the forests of southern Europe. Systematic cultivation of button mushrooms began in France in the eighteenth century. Today the button is the most widely grown mushroom type in the world.

I have developed this recipe with reference to James L. Matterer's *Gode Cookery* (www.godecookery.com) and The Oulu Medieval Association.

Stewed Onions with Raisins and Egg

6 medium-sized onions

115 g (¾ cup) raisins

1 tsp coarse-ground black pepper

1½–2 tbsp sugar

approx. 1 tsp salt

2 egg yolks

2 tbsp apple cider vinegar

Quarter the onions and place in a pan together with the raisins. Add just enough water to barely cover the onions. Bring to a boil, skimming off any surface foam during cooking. After 20–30 minutes, when the onions are cooked, add the pepper, sugar and salt. Combine the egg yolks and vinegar and add to the pan. Stir over a moderate heat for a short while, until the eggs have coagulated. This is a delicious recipe from *The Good Huswifes Jewell*, from sixteenth-century England. The dish can be eaten on its own or together with meat.

I have developed this recipe from The Oulu Medieval Association's collection of medieval recipes.

Meat

English Lamb Stew

800–900 g (1 lb 12 oz–2 lb) boneless mutton or lamb
400 ml (1¾ cups) water
1 cube chicken bouillon
2 chopped onions
1 tsp chopped fresh parsley
1 tsp chopped fresh rosemary
1 tsp chopped fresh thyme
1 tsp chopped fresh marjoram or savory
½ tsp ground ginger
½ tsp ground caraway
½ tsp ground coriander
salt to taste
250 ml (1¼ cups) white wine
2 eggs
2 tbsp lemon juice

Cut the meat into 2-cm cubes. Bring the water to a boil, and then add the chicken bouillon cube and cubed meat. Let it boil, skimming off any surface foam. Add the onions, herbs, spices, salt and wine. Reduce the heat, cover and leave to simmer for approximately 1½ hours.

94 Sheep in winter shelter in the Duke of Berry's book of hours (1416). Sheep are among the oldest domestic animals known to mankind, and have often been described as helpless and dull-witted. In times gone by sheep symbolized innocence and sincerity as well, but depictions of them could also allude to a person easily led and lured by others.

In a bowl, mix the eggs with the lemon juice. Remove the stew from the heat and carefully add the egg mixture. Serve. This recipe is taken from the *Forme of Cury*, with reference to Maggie Black's *The Medieval Cookbook*.

In the Middle Ages sheep were highly valued, since they provided milk and wool in addition to meat. Italy was among the most important wool-exporting countries in Europe, with mutton enough for poorer tables as well. Despite the English also being large-scale producers of wool, mutton was not an upper-class delicacy in England: the meat from English sheep was tough, since the animals travelled long distances while pastured on the hills and stretches of high moorland.

Roasted Paupiettes of Veal with Bacon and Herbs

400–600 g (14 oz–1 lb 5 oz) veal
1 tsp salt
2 tsp ground fennel
2 tsp ground marjoram
3 tbsp chopped fresh parsley
6–8 slices bacon
3 tbsp chopped fresh thyme
2 tsp ground basil

Cut the veal into four long strips, pound them thin and arrange them alongside each other in a baking dish. Sprinkle with the salt, fennel, marjoram and chopped fresh parsley. Chop the bacon finely and distribute it over the seasoned veal strips together with the basil and fresh chopped thyme, and roll the strips into paupiettes. Bake in a hot oven for 20–25 minutes or grill on an open fire until the meat is cooked.

Since veal is not always readily available, it can be replaced with minute steaks cut from the outer fillet of beef. The original recipe dates from fifteenth-century Italy (Platina VI).

Pork Meatballs with Currants

1 kg (2 lb 3 oz) pork
1 litre (2 pints) beef stock
1 portion almond milk (recipe on p. 186)
6 tbsp currants
½ tsp ground nutmeg
¼ tsp ground cloves
½ tsp ground black pepper
salt
2–4 eggs
oil or butter for frying

to decorate:
almond milk, sugar, nutmeg, edible violets

Cube the pork and cook in the beef stock until almost done, although still slightly pink inside. Strain, reserving the stock. Measure just under half the stock into a saucepan and prepare the almond milk. Cut the pork cubes into smaller pieces and mince in a food processor together with the currants and spices. Shape into balls and brown in oil or butter in a frying pan. Place the meatballs onto a serving platter and pour some of the cooking liquid and almond milk mixture on top. Finally sprinkle with sugar and a hint of nutmeg, and decorate with fresh violets.

You may wish to work a few eggs into the minced meat paste, in order to better retain the shape of the meatballs during frying. This recipe is based on the cooking instructions of a fifteenth-century English manuscript (Harleian MS 279) and was also developed by Maggie Black.

Chicken in Red Wine Sauce

1 whole chicken
200 ml (1 cup) chicken stock
200 ml (1 cup) red wine
1 tbsp red wine vinegar
¼ tsp ground cloves
¼ tsp ground nutmeg

S. esprit

D omine labia mea aperies. Et os meū annūciab' laudtiā. ❧ eus in adiutoriū intende. Dñe ad adiuuandū me festina. ❧ lor patri et filio et spū sctō. Sic erat in prīcipe et nc et semp et in secla sclōz ā atta. hijc.

½ tsp ground black pepper
1 tsp ground cinnamon
white bread
sugar or honey

R oast the bird in the oven until well done and cut it into portions or bite-sized pieces. Combine the chicken stock, red wine, vinegar and spices and heat in a saucepan or frying pan, taking care not to boil it. Cut some bread into pieces and add to the broth until the desired thickness is obtained. You can pass a hand mixer through the preparation to render it smooth. Add sugar or honey to taste. Add the chicken parts or pieces and leave to simmer for 10 minutes over a moderate heat.

You can also pan fry shop-bought chicken strips and add them to the sauce, or serve the sauce separately. This *Gelyne in Dubette* recipe originates in fifteenth century England (Harleian MS 279). Sources include *Take a Thousand Eggs or More*, fifteenth-century, England and The Oulu Medieval Association's recipe collection.

Saracen Chicken with Sweetmeats

1 roasted chicken (not overcooked) or 500 g (1 lb) chicken fillet strips
(optional: 1 chicken liver)
50 g (2 oz) scalded almonds
50 g (2 oz) raisins
10 dried dates, pitted
10 prunes, pitted
2 slices white bread
approx. 300 ml (1¼ cups) white wine
juice of ½ lemon
juice of 1 orange
1 apple
1 pear
2 slices bacon
1 tsp salt

opposite: 95 Cockerels, hazel grouse and other birds in a miniature from 1290. Europe's domestic chickens descend from the red junglefowl (*Gallus gallus*) of Southeast Asia. In 500 BC the Persians returned with fighting cocks from their military expeditions to the East. Initially hens and roosters were primarily used for religious or sport-related purposes. After the food ban was lifted, the fowl long remained mostly poor-man's fare. During the Roman Empire the breeding and consumption of chickens increased noticeably, and at the beginning of the 2nd century they were already quite common domestic fowl in Europe.

spice mix:
¼ tsp ground nutmeg
¾ tsp ground black pepper
¾ tsp ground ginger
¼ tsp ground cloves

Toast the bread and cut it into pieces. Juice the lemon and orange and combine with the wine. Peel and dice the apple and the pear. Cut up the prunes and dried dates. Cut the bacon into thin strips and the roasted chicken into bite-sized pieces.

Bake the liver in the oven or pan-fry it in oil. In a food processor, mince the liver together with the toasted pieces of bread, spices and juice and wine concoction. Poor the preparation into a frying pan or saucepan and add the chicken pieces, fresh and dried fruits, raisins, almonds and bacon. Bring to a boil and leave to simmer over a moderate heat for 15–20 minutes. If the liquid evaporates, add more wine. Before serving, taste and add seasoning as needed.

This *Saracen Brodo* recipe dates from fourteenth-century Italy, from *Libro della cucina del secolo* XIV, ed. Franceso Zambrini, and was developed by Odile Redon, Françoise Sabban and Silvano Serventi in *The Medieval Kitchen*. It recommends roasted capon, which today's busy chef can replace with a roasted chicken or pan-fried chicken fillet strips. The liver can be omitted. In the Middle Ages the function of liver in food preparation was to act as a binding agent, although the final product will not suffer too badly without it.

Jacobean Layered Chicken with Cheese

4 whole roasted chickens
slices of white bread
Gouda cheese
6 tbsp cane sugar
1 litre (2 pints) beef stock

Debone the chickens and divide into pieces. Bring the beef stock to a boil in a saucepan. Arrange some slices of bread in an ovenproof dish and layer them with four slices of Gouda cheese, chicken pieces and sugar. Repeat, making a total of six similar layers, and pour the boiling beeſ stock on top of everything. The stock will soften the bread and melt the cheese. Serve the dish hot. This is an easy recipe that will feed twelve.

This Flemish recipe dates from the first quarter of the sixteenth century (University of Ghent, MS 476), and I have also used Ria Jansen-Sieben and Johanna Maria van Winter, eds, *De keuken van de late middeleeuwen*. It calls for spit-roasted chicken, which, for the sake of simplicity, can be replaced with oven-roasted chicken.

Partridge in Ginger Sauce

3 partridges
pinch of ground cloves
pinch of ground mace
1 litre (2 pints) beef stock
150 ml (½ cup) red wine
1 tsp whole black peppercorns
2 hard-boiled egg yolks
¼ tsp ground ginger
pinch of ground saffron
salt
6 slices toasted bread

Place a small amount of ground cloves and nutmeg into each bird, and tie the legs together, provided these have not been removed. Bring the beef stock to a boil and add the partridges, black peppercorns and wine. Do not allow vigorous boiling. Skim off any surface foam during the next five minutes, then cover with a lid and leave to simmer for 20 minutes. Once the birds are soft, remove them from the saucepan and cut them lengthwise into halves. Reserve the cooking liquid.

In a dish, place each half on top of a slice of bread, and store in a warm place such as the oven. In a bowl, blend the boiled egg yolks, ginger, saffron, salt and a suitable amount of the cooking liquid into a sauce, and pour it over the birds. Serve. Rowanberry or cranberry jelly, for instance, will enhance the overall flavour magnificently. The original recipe belongs to an English manuscript collection (Harleian MS 4016) and has also been developed by Moira Buxton in *Medieval Cooking Today*.

96 Owing to their large numbers, hares and rabbits were part of the tables of the lower classes as well. The medieval physicians believed that the consumption of hare meat could cause sleeplessness and a sense of melancholy. *Tacuinum sanitatis*, a popular manual on maintenance of health, noted that the consumption of hare was beneficial particularly in the winter season and in cold regions, and to overweight persons or those who were endowed with cold distinctive properties. The hare was also the subject of scores of past myths and beliefs, such as being taken for an androgynous creature that changed gender during the course of its lifetime. The hare's exaggerated predisposition to copulate made it a symbol of lustfulness; on the other hand, in Christian iconography, a white rabbit perched at the feet of the Virgin Mary delineated victory over carnality and lust. Elsewhere it might have alluded to a God-fearing person, and rabbits nibbling on grapevines indicated those who had gained entrance into paradise. Just like the Easter egg, the Easter rabbit was the symbol of fruitfulness and new life.

Parisian Hare Stew

1 hare (approx. 1½ kg or 3½ lb)
3 onions
1 tbsp butter or lard for frying
2 slices wheat bread
500 ml (1 pint) beef stock
150 ml (½ cup) red wine
150 ml (½ cup) red wine vinegar
juice of ½ lemon
2 tsp water
1 tsp ground ginger
(optional. ½ tsp grains of paradise)
2 whole cloves, crushed
1 tsp ground black pepper
½ tsp ground nutmeg
1 tsp ground cinnamon
salt

You can use either a fresh or frozen hare. Toast the bread slices, crumble them into a bowl and pour the red wine, vinegar and one-fifth of the beef stock on top. Cut the hare meat into bite-sized pieces and brown them in the oven on the top rack under the grill. Chop the onions and brown them in butter or lard in a frying pan. Add the pieces of hare and continue browning for a couple of minutes. Combine the seasoning, lemon juice and water. Mash the moistened bread with a fork and add the remainder of the beef stock to the bowl. Mix well. For a smoother texture, press the mixture through a sieve with the help of a spoon, or use a hand mixer. Add the bread and spice mixtures to the frying pan and cover with a lid. Simmer over a moderate heat for about two hours or until the meat is tender. Taste and add salt and seasoning if needed.

My fellow historians have also included a pinch of ground cardamom and coriander in this aromatic pottage. You can, for instance, serve it with rowanberry jelly, Tuscan wild mushrooms (p. 159) and spelt frumenty (p. 151). The recipe dates from late fourteenth-century France, from the *Ménagier de Paris*, an anonymous household guidebook. I developed it with reference to Odile Redon, Françoise Sabban and Silvano Serventi, *The*

Medieval Kitchen. In the original version, the hare is first spit-roasted and then cut up for pan-frying.

Venison Pie

crust:
300 g (10½ oz) butter
275 g (10 oz) medium-coarse wheat flour
1 tsp baking powder
200 ml (1 cup) water

filling:
1 kg (2 lb 3 oz) venison (use fallow or red deer)
3 tbsp honey
4 egg yolks
2 slices bacon
1 tsp salt
½ tsp ground black pepper
½ tsp ground ginger
(1 egg yolk for glazing)

Prepare the piecrust: combine the butter, flour and baking powder into a crumbly paste and add the water. Work the dough by hand until even, but do not knead. Divide the dough into two equal parts, press each half into a rectangular shape and place in the refrigerator to cool for a while before rolling it out and folding it a few times to obtain a flaky dough.

Cook the meat in just enough salted water to cover it. Mince the cooked meat in a food processor. Fry the bacon and cut it into tiny pieces. Combine all the ingredients for the filling.

Roll out one half of the dough into a rectangular sheet approximately 28 x 38 cm and place onto a baking tray lined with baking parchment. Spread the pie filling on top. Roll out the other half of the dough into a matching sheet, place it over the filling and fold the edges of the bottom layer over the top, closing the pie carefully. Pierce the top layer here and there with a fork; if you wish, you can glaze it with egg yolk. You can also give the pie a festive look by moulding some of the dough into ribbons or leaves, which you add to the top layer, glazing the decorations as well. Bake the pie on the bottom rack of a 200°C (390°F) oven for approximately 30 minutes, until the top has taken some colour.

This recipe is based on a fifteenth-century English manuscript (Harleian MS 279). You can use the meat of either fallow deer or red deer. If you prefer not to make your own pastry, you can use ready-made flaky pastry sheets (approx. 800 g or 1 lb 12 oz).

Fish

Salmon Pie with Sweetmeats

base:
either ½ batch shortcrust pastry dough (see p. 172) or 500 g (1 lb) ready-made, uncooked shortcrust pastry

filling:
250–300 ml (1–1 ¼ cups) white wine
½ tsp salt
400–500 g (around 1 lb) salmon cut in strips
4–6 tbsp dried figs
¼ tsp ground white pepper
½ tsp ground cinnamon
¼ tsp ground cloves
¼ tsp ground nutmeg
½ tsp ground ginger
pinch of ground saffron
1–2 tbsp pine nuts
2 tbsp currants
¼ tsp salt
5–6 tbsp dried dates
approx. 3 tbsp almond milk (recipe on p. 186)

Prepare the dough and divide it into two halves. Cut the figs into small pieces, place in a saucepan and add around a third of the white wine. Cook for 15 minutes or until soft, let cool and process with a hand mixer

The Glory and the Cruelty of the Hunt

The large number of medieval hunting guides bears testimony to the popularity of the pursuit. The handbooks of the era described different types of game and the methods for catching them, while the accompanying illustrations introduced a multitude of approaches as well as implements such as swords, longbows, spears and traps.

The best-known hunting book is Gaston Phoebus's *Livre de chasse*. Of the text, composed in 1387–9, 37 illustrated manuscript copies still remain, the most beautiful of which can be found in the collections of the National Library of France. Other noteworthy hunting manuals are *De arte venandi*, a treatise on falconry by the Frederick II (1194–1250), and the *Livre du roy Modus* (1354–76) attributed to Henri de Ferrières.

Hunting manuals were compiled for the upper classes, and their objective was to reflect the opinions, values and ideals of those who had commissioned them. As a result their authors paid tribute to the many fine aspects of the hunt: Alfonso X of Castile wrote in his thirteenth-century statutory code *Partidas* that all forms of hunting were for the good of man, since they 'helped to ease the burden of evil thoughts'. Hunting was a salubrious occupation, since the physical activity associated with the pursuit — provided there was enough of it — generated a healthy appetite and the ability to sleep soundly, the two most precious things in a person's life. The Spanish writer Juan Manuel stated in his *Libro de los estados* that the hunter learned to endure great physical exertion and to know the roads and pathways of his surroundings well, thus becoming generally more generous and forthright.

According to Gaston Phoebus, the true hunter eschewed idleness, which was the source of wicked and sinful behaviour of the highest degree. The hunter was kept busy from dawn 'til dusk, enjoying life to the fullest: the fresh morning air, the sound of birdsong, the glistening of dewdrops on leaves and grass. He got more out of life than others, in addition to which, after death, he gained direct access to Paradise. Furthermore the hunter lived longer, since he ate and drank in moderation. He took much exercise, either on foot or on horseback, an activity that enabled him to exude harmful bodily fluids and keep well.

Yet blood sports had their critics, too. Erasmus of Rotterdam, who already loathed the arrogant lifestyle of the aristocracy, ridiculed the high-born hunters and their deer-cutting rituals in his work *The Praise of Folly* (*Moriae Encomium*, 1509). Erasmus's friend Thomas More was

97 Unmaking a deer, from Gaston Phoebus' hunting manual, *Livre de chasse* (1337–8).

particularly concerned about the cruel aspects of hunting. In his *Utopia* (1516), More wrote that the Utopians had rejected hunting, counting the pursuit 'the lowest, the vilest, and most abject part of butchery'. He went on to say that butchers killed their victims for reasons of necessity, while a hunter only sought gratification in the slaughter and murder of an innocent and frightened animal. In blood sports More saw traits of sadistic amusement and the sinful enjoyment of killing for the sake of it.

Other contemporaries, however, had a higher opinion of hunters than of ordinary butchers. The death of a free animal in the wild was nobler and less to be pitied than that of a defenceless, tame and trusting slaughterhouse beast.

98 Salmon fishing in the North.

until smooth. Cut the dates into small pieces and parboil for approximately 5 minutes in the rest of the white wine together with the salmon strips and ½ tsp salt. Strain the wine broth and reserve.

To make the fig purée, add the currants, salt and spices. Stir well and dilute the mixture as needed with the reserved wine broth. Press one half of the pie dough into a round pie dish (25–27 cm or 9–10 inches diameter), covering the bottom and sides. Spread the seasoned fig mixture evenly onto the bottom and sprinkle with pine nuts. Add the salmon and date mixture, distributing it evenly. Roll out the other half of the dough and place over the filling. Brush the top with almond milk seasoned with a pinch of ground saffron, and prick it with a fork. Bake on the lower rack of a 200°C (390°F) oven for 35–40 minutes or until the top of the pie has risen and turned a pretty golden colour.

This is a fifteenth-century English recipe (Harleian MS 4016):

Tart de ffruyte. Take figges, and seth hem in wyne, and grinde hem smale. And take hem vppe into a vessell; And take pouder peper, Canell, Clowes, Maces, pouder ginger, pynes, grete reysouns of couraunce, saffroñ, and salte, and cast thereto; and Peñ make faire lowe coffyns, and couche Þis stuff there-iñ, and plonte pynes aboue; and kut dates and fressh salmoñ in faire peces, or elles fressh eles, and parboyle hem a litull in wyne, and couche thereon; And couche the coffyns faire with Þe same paaste, and endore the coffyñ withoute with saffron & almond mylke; and set hem in Þe oveñ and lete bake.

Baked Pike with White Wine Sauce

1 pike
1–2 slices white bread
150 ml (5 fl. oz) sweet white wine

1 tbsp vinegar
⅓ tsp ground pepper
½ tsp ground ginger
salt (to taste)
sugar (to taste)

Remove the crust from the bread, cut the soft parts into pieces and place in a bowl. Add the wine and vinegar, stir and press the mixture through a colander, or process with a hand mixer. Pour the mixture into a saucepan, add the pepper, bring to a boil and gently simmer over a moderate heat for 15 minutes or until thickened. Bake the pike in the oven or pan fry it in oil. Add the ginger, salt and sugar to the sauce. When the fish is fully cooked, transfer it to a serving platter and pour the sauce on top. Serve. By adding a pinch of ground saffron to the sauce, you will give it a golden colour.

This recipe originates in fifteenth-century England, from *Take a Thousand Eggs or More*. The pike was held in high esteem in the Middle Ages. From the papal court in Avignon in the 1330s, delegations were dispatched on a regular basis to faraway locations in search of pike, extending into Burgundy, Lyon and the upper runs of the Rhone. Fish cages were hooked to riverboats to store the catch and keep it fresh, and the pike were fed small fish to keep them alive. In the Nordic countries a selection of small, whole stockfish, dried pike heads and bits of stockfish derived from pike formed a veritable gentleman's treat. In the sixteenth century lutefisk was made from dried pike for the fast of Christmas Eve.

Fried Fish with Fruit Compote

500 g (1 lb) fish (tench or similar)
oil for frying
1–2 slices white bread
75 ml (2½ fl. oz) red wine
1 tbsp red wine vinegar
4 tbsp dried figs, chopped
4 tbsp onion, chopped
4 tbsp shelled almonds

4 tbsp currants
⅛ tsp ground cloves
½ tsp ground ginger
1 tsp ground cinnamon
1 tbsp sugar

Fry the fish in oil until well done. Remove the crust from the bread, cut the soft parts into pieces, place in a pan and work in the wine, vinegar and sugar. Add the chopped figs. Sauté the chopped onions and almonds, and add them to the bread mixture together with the spices and currants. Bring to a boil. Place the cooked fish onto a platter, cover it with the compote and serve hot or cold.

If you do not care for acidic flavours, leave out the vinegar.

The above recipe originates in fifteenth-century England, from *Ancient Cookery* via David Friedman and Elizabeth Cook's *Cariadoc's Miscellany*. It suggests tench, a fish of the carp family, although pike, whitefish or bream are good alternatives.

Fried Fish Fillets in Sweet-and-Sour Sauce

fresh fish fillets (haddock or similar)
olive oil for frying

sauce:
300 ml (10 fl. oz) red wine vinegar
3 tbsp sugar
1 onion, chopped
½ tsp ground mace
½ tsp ground cloves
1 tsp ground black pepper

In a frying pan, combine the red wine vinegar, sugar, chopped onion and spices. Taste and adjust the sweetness and the spices to find a good balance between the sweet and sour flavours. Bring to a boil, lower the heat and simmer until the onions are soft. In another pan, fry the fish fillets on both sides in olive oil until pale brown, transfer into a serving dish and pour the sauce on top.

This recipe originates in fourteenth-century England (*Utilis Coquinario*). Constance B. Hieatt and Sharon Butler's *Curye on Inglish* recommends haddock, but other similar fish will also do.

An Italian recipe of the same era is more elaborate:

800 g (1¾ lb) firm-fleshed fish
olive oil
2–4 onions, chopped
100 g (3½ oz) shelled almonds
100 g (3½ oz) raisins
20 prunes, pitted and chopped
150 ml (5 fl. oz) sweet white wine
3 tbsp vinegar
pinch of ground saffron
½ tsp ground black pepper
⅓ tsp ground ginger
½ tsp ground cardamom
salt
sugar

Cube the fish and fry it in olive oil until well done. Set aside the pieces. In the same oil, sauté the chopped onions until tender; add the almonds, raisins, chopped prunes, spices and salt. Stir and add the wine and vinegar, and let simmer for 20 minutes. Taste the flavour and add sugar if not sufficiently sweet. Add the fish. Serve.

The sources for this recipe are *Libro della cucina del secolo XIV*, ed. Francesco Zambrini; and Odile Redon, François Sabban and Silvano Serventi, *The Medieval Kitchen*.

Poached Fish with Caraway Sauce

fresh fish
200 ml (1 cup) almond milk (recipe on p. 186)
1 slice white bread
¼ tsp ground ginger
½ tsp ground caraway seeds

pinch of ground saffron
(optional: salt)

Poach the fish or cook it using any other cooking method. Measure the almond milk into a bowl and add the soft inside of the bread. Stir in the spices and pass the sauce through a colander, or process it in a hand mixer until smooth. Place in a saucepan and cook for a short while, stirring. Taste and add salt if needed. Place the fish in a serving dish and pour the sauce on top. Serve.

This recipe is taken from the fifteenth-century French culinary work, *Vivendier*:

> *Pour faire une comminee de poisson: prenez du lait d'amandes et du pain blancq trempé dedens sans rostir, commin, gingembre et saffren; passez tout parmy l'estamine, faictez bouillir une onde; qui ne soit trop cler ne trop espés; et jettez par dessus vostre poisson, quel qu'il soit.*

Caraway is a member of the parsley family. It is native to the region around the Black Sea, but was cultivated in prehistoric times in different parts of Europe. The caraway seeds known to us (Latin *Carum carvi*, from the Arabic *karawiya*) are different from the cumin, or *jeera*, used in Indian cooking. In

99 Salted, dried and smoked fish in Olaus Magnus's work. Herring in all its forms was the signature fish of the Middle Ages. It was eaten salted, smoked or dried, or enjoyed fresh in garlic sauce. Since herrings did not thrive in warm waters, they were exported south from the northern regions. Herrings were shipped salted to the warmth of Italy from Scandinavia, and sent salted and smoked, or kippered, from England. Herring is not often mentioned in medieval cookery books, although it appears occasionally on the menus of the upper classes. For the fast of Christmas in 1520, the dining table of Hans Brask (1464–1538), Bishop of Linköping in Sweden, paraded smoked salmon, fried herring, eel in mustard sauce, lutefisk with raisins and almonds, Skåne herring, poached young herring, poached fresh fish with fish sauce, ling in oil, assorted other saltwater fish, dried, unsalted pike from Finland, fried fish, Norrbotten salmon, and apples and nuts.

Roman times soldiers chewed caraway seeds to freshen their breath and expedite the digestion. The Egyptians added caraway to the blend of spices used for the mummification of their dead, as it was thought to protect against evil spirits. In the Middle Ages the roots of the plant could be used for soup. In Norway caraway soup made from the roots and leaves of caraway is still a well-known dish today.

Baked Eel in Red Wine

1 kg (2 lb 3 oz) eel
salt
ground saffron
ground black pepper
red wine

If you are using a whole eel, skin, clean and cut it into individual portions. Arrange the pieces in an ovenproof dish and sprinkle with salt, pepper and saffron. Add just enough wine to cover the pieces. Cover the dish and cook in a 180°C (355°F) oven for 30–45 minutes or until the pieces are cooked through and feel soft when pressed with a fork. Serve. This recipe is taken from a fifteenth-century English manuscript (Harley MS 5401). Sources include James L. Matterer's *Gode Cookery* and Constance B. Hieatt, *The Middle English Culinary Recipes in* MS *Harley 5401: An Edition and Commentary*.

Eels were preferably fried or baked in medieval times, a method which reduced their natural moistness. Black pepper had extremely dry and warm properties and was therefore well suited to eels. Certain experts were of the opinion that eels should be killed by submersion in salt for the removal of any superfluous cold and moist properties. The river lamprey, on the other hand, was better drowned in wine, after which, ideally, it was to be parboiled twice in wine, then baked and seasoned with warm and dry herbs and spices.

The eel puzzled people of the past: why was there no spawn or milt to be found of this freshwater fish? Aristotle (384–322 BC), the ancient Greek philosopher and authority on many subjects, who was highly regarded in the Middle Ages, surmised that the offspring of eels issued from the bowels of the earth. For his part, the Roman naturalist Pliny the Elder (AD 23–79) believed eels to be born out of the shreds of eel skin that came off whenever a fully-grown eel rubbed against stones. The thirteenth-century author of the *Ashmole Bestiary* described eels 30 feet long inhabiting the River Ganges, and stated that if a human drank the wine in which an eel had drowned, he would never again be able to partake of the beverage in question. He also said that eels were born out of mud.

The riddle of the eel did not unravel until the early twentieth century: the creatures migrate to spawn in the deep seawaters of the western rim of the Atlantic Ocean. The Gulf Stream carries the hatched larvae back to the coasts of Europe, where they undergo a metamorphosis and travel up to their freshwater habitats.

Sauces and spices

Cameline Sauce

1–2 slices white bread
275 ml (9 fl. oz) white wine
1–2 tbsp wine vinegar
1 tsp ground cinnamon
½ tsp ground ginger
½ tsp ground cloves
⅛ tsp ground nutmeg
¼ tsp ground black pepper
pinch of ground saffron
2 tbsp brown sugar
salt

Toast the bread until brown, cut it into pieces and put to soak in the wine and vinegar. Press the softened mixture through a sieve or mix it with a hand mixer until smooth. Add the spices and, if you wish, the brown sugar and a tiny amount of salt. Taste. The flavour of cinnamon should be dominant. Serve the sauce with meat or fish, either cold or heated in a saucepan.

This recipe is based on the cooking instructions from the mid-fifteenth-century French culinary manuscript *Vivendier*. There were several versions of *cameline* sauce, of which the cooked ones were recommended especially in the winter.

flabellum

Gelatina

Gallatina.

Nature. f. 2. s. melior excea. sparata cū pull coliībis. Iuuamētuū collere. nocumētuz. nennis z melācolie remotio noā. cū uino re centi odonfeio.

100 Galentine sauce served with fowl in Abu Khasim's *Observations sur la nature et les proprietés des aliments* (1390).

Galentine Sauce

piece of white bread
3 tbsp wine vinegar
pinch of ground galangal
pinch of ground cinnamon
pinch of ground ginger
salt

Cut the soft part of the bread into pieces and combine with the vinegar and spices. Press the mixture through a sieve or mix it with a hand mixer until smooth. Add the salt. If needed, add more liquid. Serve the sauce with meat, fish or fowl. Both fresh and dried galangal can be found in shops specializing in Indian or Asian food, or in other well-stocked food stores. If you serve the sauce with fish, you can add onion and a pinch of pepper.

The original fourteenth-century recipe in the *Forme of Cury* reads as follows:

Galyntyne. Take crustes of brede and grynde hem smale. Do perto powdour of galyngale, of canel, of gynguer, and salt it; temper it vp with vyneger, and drawe it vp purgh a straynour, & messe it forth.

Cinnamon (*Cinnamomum zeylanicum*) is derived from the dried bark of the young shoots of a tree native to Sri Lanka and its neighbouring regions. Cassia (also Chinese cinnamon or bastard cinnamon, in Latin, *Cinnamomum cassia*) is a tree closely related to cinnamon and native to Burma and Southeast Asia. In the Middle Ages the distinction between cinnamon and cassia was not always obvious, and in Europe, the two were sold as one and the same spice.

Jance Sauce

6 tbsp ground almonds
2 pieces white bread
approx. 450 ml (15 fl. oz) white wine
1–2 tsp lemon juice
3 cloves garlic, pressed
½ tsp ground ginger
½ tsp ground grains of paradise (see p. 187)

Crumble the soft part of the bread and moisten it with one-third of the white wine. Add the ground almonds and garlic. Add the spices and ½ tsp salt, and press the mixture through a sieve or mix it with a hand mixer until smooth. Add the remainder of the wine. Cook over a moderate heat for about 10 minutes. Remove from the heat and stir in the lemon juice.

This recipe is based on Maître Chiquart's instructions for a sauce suitable for capon in *Du fait de cuysine*, so it should be served with chicken. It was also developed by David Friedman and Elizabeth Cook in *Cariadoc's Miscellany*.

Garlic Sauce

6 egg yolks

1½ tbsp vinegar

½ tbsp water

3 cloves garlic

1 tsp salt

Peel and crush the cloves of garlic. Combine all ingredients and cook over a moderate heat for approximately five minutes, stirring continuously. This sauce is well suited to chicken. This recipe originates in *Ein Buch von Guter Spise* from mid-fourteenth-century Germany.

Good All-round Sauce

400–500 ml (¾–1 pint) chicken stock

150 ml (5 fl. oz) beef stock

approx. 6 tbsp croutons

½ tsp ground pepper

½ tsp ground caraway

pinch of ground saffron

salt

Combine the chicken and beef stocks, bring to a boil, add the croutons and spices and bring to a boil once more. Lower the heat and let simmer for a short while. Remove from the hob, strain and use immediately or refrigerate for future use. This sauce originates in fifteenth-century

England, in the *Noble Boke off Cookryn*, and was also developed by William Edward Mead in *The English Medieval Feast*.

Pepper Sauce

2 slices white bread
6 chicken or other bird livers
3 tbsp red wine
approx. 3 tbsp chicken stock
pinch of ground cinnamon
pinch of ground nutmeg
pinch of ground black pepper
touch of ground saffron
salt

Fry the livers thoroughly in a frying pan or bake them in the oven, then mince them in a food processor. Toast the bread and cut it into pieces. In a bowl, combine the bread, liver, spices, wine and stock. Pass the mixture through a sieve, or mix it with a hand mixer until smooth. If necessary, the sauce can be thinned with more chicken stock. Serve with fish, meat or game.

If you wish, you can add some sugar to the sauce. This recipe for *pevrada* sauce originates in fourteenth-century Italy, from *Libro della cucina del secolo XIV*, ed. Franceso Zambrini, and another source is Odile Redon, Françoise Sabban and Silvano Serventi, *The Medieval Kitchen*.

Almond Milk

90 g (¾ cup) ground almonds
400 ml (13½ fl. oz) water
2–3 tbsp sugar
⅓ tsp salt

Bring the water to a boil in a saucepan, and add the ground almonds, sugar and salt. Simmer over a moderate heat for 15 minutes, stirring occasionally. Strain.

This recipe is based on a fourteenth-century rendition by Taillevent, *Le Viandier*. If you cannot find ready-made ground almonds, you can use

101 Collecting pepper in the East in a 15th-century miniature. Pepper (*Piper nigrum*) is derived from the drupes of a flowering vine native to the coastal regions of India. Black pepper was made from the still-green clusters of berries that were picked and dried in the sun, while white pepper was extracted from the ripened drupes, from which the red-coloured skin had been soaked off. Green pepper was still unheard of in the Middle Ages. The presence of the word 'pepper' in the names of many spices can cause confusion. Long pepper (*Piper longum*) is only related to the pepper plant, although reminiscent of black pepper to the taste. It is also a native of India, but by the 19th century it was no longer brought to Europe on any significant scale. Allspice (*Pimenta dioica*), also known as Jamaica pepper or myrtle pepper, belongs to the family of myrtle plants (*Myrtaceae*), while rose pepper, in turn, is the dried berry of a South American tree. Chilli is a generic term for a variety of capsicums, the cultivated forms of which include sweet peppers and chilli peppers, neither of which were known in the Middle Ages. Anise pepper (*Zanthoxylum piperitum*), also known as Sichuan pepper or Japanese pepper, is the dried berry of a tree of the rue family. Melegueta pepper (*Aframomum melegueta* of the genus Amomum), commonly known as grains of paradise in the Middle Ages, is a plant related to ginger and turmeric. In the Nordic countries grains of paradise may be hard to come by when called for in medieval recipes, but elsewhere in Europe the spice is more common. In England it is also called alligator pepper or Guinea grains; in France, *graines de paradis, maniguette or poivre de Guinée*; in Spain, *malagueta*; and in Germany, *Malagettapfeffer*.

102 A bride and her retinue at table: wine and bird pasties are being served. Sophisticated meals at court often finished with the sampling of spices.

whole, shelled almonds. Crush them in a mortar as finely as possible, and once they have simmered, pass a hand mixer through the mixture to better incorporate the almonds into the liquid for a fuller result. Strain the mixture.

Postprandial Parlour Spices

anise

caraway

Place anise and caraway seeds onto a serving platter. If you wish, you can decorate with edible silver beads. Serve the spices together with hippocras at the end of the meal (recipe on p. 208). Fennel seeds are also excellent postprandial spices.

Traditional Blend of Spices

1 tsp ground black pepper

1 tsp ground cinnamon

1 tsp ground ginger

¼ tsp ground saffron

⅛ tsp ground cloves

This is a traditional medieval blend of spices suitable for most dishes. You can also make a larger portion to have on hand in your spice cupboard.

Milk and Egg dishes

Brie with Herbs and Nuts

300 g (10½ oz) Brie

100 g (3½ oz) crème fraîche

50 g (1¾ oz) nuts

1 tbsp chopped parsley

1 tbsp chopped chives

1 tbsp chopped thyme

1 clove garlic, crushed

1 tbsp lemon juice

salt

pepper

He who wished to become a chef in the Middle Ages had to work his way up a structured system of apprenticeship, as was the case in other medieval professions. In France chefs formed a professional organization earlier than elsewhere, and in his 1268 *Book of the Trades* (*Livre des métiers*), Provost Étienne Boileau refers to the statutes of the Parisian guild of master chefs. In England chefs did not organize themselves professionally until the late fifteenth century. It has been debated whether women were allowed to practise as professional chefs in the Middle Ages, as any clear-cut references to female members of the trade are yet to be discovered. The status of an ordinary chef was not elevated. To give an example, in thirteenth-century Genoa a chef's salary was relatively low and his profession was not coveted — master chefs to a royal court, on the other hand, were an altogether different matter.

Those professionally engaged in cooking were often ridiculed. It was partly a question of the sceptical attitude people in the Middle Ages assumed towards any profession associated with the handling of blood and the combining and converting of different ingredients — in other words, transforming the God-given order of things. Particularly in substitute dishes, certain ingredients were completely disguised as something else. Cooks were closely associated with other unpleasant skilled workers such as butchers, alchemists and dyers.

The most celebrated chef of the Middle Ages is undoubtedly Guillaume Tirel (*c.* 1310–1395), known as Taillevent. He served as master chef, or *maître queux*, at the royal courts of Charles V and Charles VI of France, and the most famous version of the French *Viandier* recipe collection has been attributed specifically to him. *Maître queux* was a royal profession abolished only at the time of the French Revolution. The word '*queux*' was derived from the Latin *coquus*, meaning

'cook'. In the manner of all royal servants, the head chef, too, proudly wore a livery trimmed in the colours of his master.

The position of head chef to a royal court was very demanding. At the Savoyard court Maître Chiquart, who served under Amadeus VIII, Duke of Savoy, in the early fifteenth century, defined his profession as science and art combined, as he was writing the cookbook *Du fait de cuisine* (*On Cookery*) by royal commission of his employer. A chef had to be thoroughly acquainted with the natural properties of the ingredients, since he needed to know what was safe to serve his patron and what required special treatment. The basic repertoire of a royal chef comprised different types of roasts, stews, sauces, soups, jellies, preserves, puddings, porridge, cakes, biscuits and pies. On account of the requisites involving fasting, chefs had to be able to conjure up skilful substitutes. These were often just as mouthwatering and impressive as the delicacies served on meat-eating days. However, the talents of a royal chef were truly put to the test when it came to producing entremets, at which point the key objective was the creation of a grand spectacle. Chefs experimented with new colours, colour combinations and designs.

Yet the head chef was not the chief authority on matters pertaining to food at a royal court. The monarch or nobleman in residence appointed a majordomo, or chamberlain, from the ranks of the aristocracy to manage the palace staff and household (in French, *maître d'hôtel*). The chamberlain was ultimately responsible for the food stores, menu planning and preparation of dishes carried out by the chefs. He also led and supervised the group of staff assigned to perform the food service, a brigade that included lackeys, keepers of spices, keepers of bread, cup-bearers, carvers, sauce-makers and bakers, among others.

In palace kitchens all tasks were assigned to professional personnel, who in turn were assisted by a large group of helpers. There was the rotisserie turner, the tableware attendant, the saucemaker, the soupmaker, the spice-grinder and the fire-poker. In middle-class or peasant households the mistress of the house and her daughters performed all these tasks themselves.

In the fifteenth century the kitchens at the Burgundian court employed two kitchen scribes to oversee in general, including the expenses, the procurement of food and the recruitment of staff. Three chefs supervised the preparation of food for the regal table, one of them the head chef, whose special emblem was a large wooden ladle. Twenty-five professional staff assisted the chefs in the food preparation, and they, in turn, were assisted by a group of non-professionals. The head chef on duty was seated between the stove and the service table, from where he had a full view of the room. He tasted soups and sauces with his large wooden ladle, at the same time ordering kitchen staff around to carry out their duties, or rebuking them for negligence. On the odd occasion, such as when the first truffles were presented, the head chef might come out in person and serve, torch in hand. The court chronicler Olivier de la Marche (1425–1502) carefully recounted all this with respect and admiration.

In the remote Nordic countries, in the Middle Ages and the early modern period, the royal castles were important administrative centres, where a manifold staff of officers, clerks and hired hands had to be fed. Even Häme Castle employed a castle chef, a cellarman, a brewer, a baker, a cooper, a pansmith, a butcher and other craftsmen and service staff. In the days of Duke John and Catherine Jagellon, Turku Castle secured the services of four master chefs, two junior chefs, four chef apprentices and a baker, a keeper of the silver and a number of footmen for the dining table of the royal couple.

Grind the nuts. In a bowl, combine the crème fraîche, lemon juice, nuts, herbs, garlic and salt and pepper. Refrigerate for one hour. Slice the Brie horizontally into two wedges of equal thickness. Spread the cream and herb mixture onto the slices, and press them together. Wrap the cheese in kitchen foil and refrigerate. Remove from the refrigerator 30 minutes before serving.

For centuries, the Brie region in northern France was a centre for Parisian cheese retailers. Charlemagne particularly enjoyed Brie de Meaux, while Duke Charles of Orléans presented his female courtiers with the cheese at New Year. I have developed this recipe with reference to Josy Marty-Dufaut's *La Gastronomie du Moyen Age*.

Gingered Cheese Pie

base:
100 g (3½ oz) butter
175 g (1¼ cups) medium-coarse wheat flour
$^1/_3$ tsp salt
2 tbsp water

filling:
3 eggs
200 g (7 oz) strong Brie
½–1 tsp ground ginger
½ tsp salt

Sift the flour and salt, add the butter and work the ingredients into a crumbly paste, using your fingertips. Last, add the water, incorporating it briskly. Press the dough onto the bottom and sides of a round pie dish. Peel and cube the Brie. In a bowl, whisk the eggs, and add the seasoning and cheese. Press the mixture through a sieve or mix it with a hand mixer for a lump-free filling. Pour the mixture onto the pie base and bake on the middle rack of a 200°C (390°F) oven until the filling has risen and browned, approximately half an hour. Let the pie cool for a moment before serving.

This recipe is based on the late fourteenth-century English cooking instructions for *Tart de Bry* in the *Forme of Cury*, and I have also used as a source Constance B. Hieatt, Brenda Hosington and Sharon Butler, *Pleyn Delit, Medieval Cookery for Modern Cooks*.

Cream Pie with Raisins and Dates

base:
125 g (4½ oz) butter
200 g (1½ cups) medium-coarse wheat flour
½ tsp salt
4 tbsp water
(optional: 1 tbsp sugar)

filling:
400 ml (13½ fl. oz) cream
6 egg whites
3 tbsp sugar
3 tbsp raisins
1½ tbsp dried, pitted dates

Using your fingertips, combine the butter, flour and salt (and sugar, if you wish the pie base to be sweet) into a crumbly paste; add the water, incorporating it briskly. Press the dough onto the bottom and sides of a cake pan with a removable bottom (20–22 cm or 8–9 inches diameter). Coat a piece of kitchen foil with butter and line the pie base, including the sides. Fill the lined base with dried peas. Blind bake the base on the middle rack of a 200°C (390°F) oven for 9 minutes. Remove the peas and kitchen foil, pierce the base with a fork here and there, and bake for an additional couple of minutes. Prepare the filling: finely chop the dates and raisins and sprinkle them onto the pie base. In a bowl, whisk the egg whites, cream and sugar, and pour the mixture onto the base. Bake on the lower rack of a 175°C (350°F) oven until

104 The manufacture of cheeses in Switzerland.

the filling has solidified and taken a pretty colour, or for approximately half an hour. Serve slightly cooled or chilled.

At medieval banquets, cream pies were served as accompaniments to main dishes; these days, however, they may be better appreciated as desserts. The above recipe is based on a sixteenth-century English source (*Proper New Booke of Cookery*, 1575) and I have also consulted The Oulu Medieval Association (*Oulun keskiaikaseura: keskiaikaisia reseptejä*). My colleagues have used a puff-pastry base, although traditional shortcrust pastry dough is likely to be better suited to this particular dish.

Apple Omelette

1 large or 2 small apples
100 ml (½ cup) water
1 tbsp butter
3 eggs
2 tsp sugar
pinch of salt
⅓ tsp ground black pepper
pinch of ground cinnamon
pinch of ground saffron

Peel and cube the apples. Place in a pan, add the water, boil for 2–3 minutes and drain the water. Melt the butter in the pan and fry the apples until they are a beautiful golden-yellow colour. In a bowl, lightly whisk the eggs together with the sugar, salt and spices. If necessary, add more butter to the frying pan before pouring in the egg mixture. Cook for a moment while stirring, then cover and leave to solidify into an omelette.

The anonymous author of the *Ménagier de Paris* advises his readers that the above *Riquemenger* recipe can be enjoyed on a piece of bread, particularly in the month of September. However, this excellent omelette is delicious on its own as well, at any time of the year.

105 A peasant's wife collects eggs, in an illustration from a 15th-century *Tacuinum*.

Poached Eggs with Mustard Sauce

sliced white bread
4 eggs
1 litre (2 pints) water
200 ml (1 cup) red wine
mustard

Heat the water and wine in a saucepan to just below boiling point. Crack an egg into a glass and pour it carefully into the barely boiling water, repeating the procedure with the remaining eggs. Gently simmer for 4–5 minutes. Using a slotted spoon, carefully lift the eggs out of the water and place them on a plate or clean towel to drain. Reserve some cooking liquid, add mustard according to taste and boil for a while, until the mixture has thickened into a sauce. Toast the bread. Place the poached eggs on the bread slices and pour the sauce over. If you like you can sprinkle the eggs with a bit of tarragon, pepper and salt.

The original version of this recipe can be found in the *Ménagier de Paris*:

Souppe en moustarde. Prenez de l'uille en quoy vous avez pochez vos oeufz, du vin, de l'eaue, et tout boulir en une paelle de fer. Puiz prenez les croustes du pain et le mettez harler sur le gril; puiz en faictes souppes quarrees et mectez boulir. Puiz retrayez vostre souppe, et mettez en ung plat ressuier. Et dedans le boullon mectez de la moustarde, et faictes boulir. Puis faictes vos souppes par escuelles, et versez vostre boullon dessus.

Poached Eggs in Golden Sauce

3 eggs
approx. 150 ml (5 fl. oz) milk
approx. 6 tbsp rice flour
several pinches of ground saffron
2 tbsp honey
(optional: salt, ground black pepper)

In a saucepan, heat the rice flour and milk to combine into a thick sauce. Add the honey and saffron, and cook over a moderate heat, stirring. In another saucepan, bring water to a boil and poach the eggs. Place the poached eggs onto a serving platter and cover with the sauce. Serve.

A spoonful of vinegar added to the water may prevent the egg whites from breaking during the cooking process. If you wish, you can also season the sauce with a pinch of salt and black pepper.

This recipe is from a fifteenth-century English manuscript (MS Harley 5401):

Popyns. Recipe clene cow mylk, & take þe flour of rice or of whete & draw þe flour with sum of þe mylk, & colour it with saferon & let it boyle, & do a lityll hony þerto; þan tak water & well it in a frying panne; þan cast in brokyn egges & fry þam hard in þe water, & lay .iij. in a dysh & þe colourd mylk þeron, & serof it forth.

106 An egg merchant. In medieval culture the egg symbolized sexuality, springtime and new life. The white colour of the eggshell was associated with purity and perfection. The chick hatching from the egg alluded to Christ risen from the grave, and eggs were therefore popular Easter decorations. The tradition of decorating Easter eggs was also known and practised: coloured eggs were hidden in gardens for children to hunt. Easter brought with it the promise of beautiful spring days, while, simultaneously, the Lenten season was coming to an end.

Golden Soup

600 ml (1¼ pints) chicken or vegetable stock

2 slices toasted, cubed white toast

2 eggs

¼ tsp ground ginger

pinch of ground galangal

½ tsp sugar

pinch of ground saffron

1 tbsp lemon juice

(optional: ½ tsp cardamom, cinnamon or coriander)

In a saucepan, bring the chicken or vegetable stock to a boil and lower the heat. Lightly toast a couple of slices of white bread and finely cube the slices. In a bowl, whisk the eggs well, add the sugar and spices and finally the hot stock, stirring constantly. Add the cubed toast and pour the mixture back into the saucepan. Reheat for a minute or two, but do not boil lest the soup curdles. Finally add the lemon juice and serve. This recipe is taken from the *Forme of Cury* and a version has also been developed by Moira Buxton in *Medieval Cooking Today*.

If you cannot find galangal, you can use ginger a little more generously. Cardamom, cinnamon and coriander are other spices suitable for this soup.

Desserts

Nucato (Spiced Honey and Nut Crunch)

750 ml (3¼ cups) honey
1 kg (2 lb 3 oz) crushed nuts or almonds
a slice of lemon for spreading the mixture

spice blend:
1 tsp ground ginger
½ tsp ground black pepper
1 tsp ground cinnamon
⅓ tsp ground cloves

In a saucepan, bring the honey to a boiling point, stirring continuously. Add the crushed nuts or almonds and 1 tsp of the spice blend. Cook over a moderate heat for 30–45 minutes, stirring frequently and taking care not to overheat the nuts or almonds lest they turn dark and bitter tasting. The concoction is ready when the nuts begin to pop. Finally stir in the remainder of the spice blend and pour the nucato onto a piece of baking parchment to cool. Smooth the surface with a slice of lemon. Refrigerate before serving. This recipe dates from fourteenth-century Italy, from *Libro della cucina del secolo XIV*, ed. Franceso Zambrini, and was also developed by Odile Redon, Françoise Sabban and Silvano Serventi in *The Medieval Kitchen*.

107 A lad thieving cherries, in a 14th-century illustration from the *Luttrell Psalter*. In Scandinavia the 1442 Land Acts of King Christopher decreed apple theft subject to pecuniary penalty. In a medieval turn of phrase, the law stated that if a thief was caught stealing apples or other fruits from another man's garden, and the farmer seized his clothing as proof, or two men testified to his identity, he was to pay a fine in the sum of three marks in indemnity to the circuit court. 'If someone fells an apple tree or a fruit tree out of someone else's garden, let him pay a fine of three marks. If he cuts a branch off the fruit tree, let him pay a fine of six pennies, if he is caught at it in the presence of witnesses.'

Spiced Pear Soup

4–5 large pears
250 ml (1 cup) beer
honey
½ tsp ground pepper
½–1 tsp ground ginger
1 tsp ground cinnamon
(optional: ½ tsp ground galangal)

Peel and cube the pears, then poach them in the beer over a moderate heat for 15–20 minutes or until soft. Liquefy with a hand mixer. Add the pepper and honey to taste. Cook over a low heat for approximately 10 minutes. Add the ginger, galangal (if desired) and cinnamon. Serve the soup warm or chilled. Before serving, sprinkle with cinnamon.

In the Middle Ages pear trees grew wild in different parts of Europe, although they were also cultivated. The earliest records of pear farming date from as far back as the fourth century BC. Pear-growing was known in the Nordic countries, too, in the Middle Ages, although the fruit fared better in temperate climates. Ripe pears were used in food and drink without too much delay, as they kept for a short time only and spoiled easily when bruised. The delicacy of the fruit also limited trading, transporting and stocking it.

I have developed this recipe with reference to Madeleine Pelner Cosman.

Cherry Pudding

500 g (1 lb) fresh cherries
200 ml (1¼ cups) red wine
180 g (¾ cup) sugar
30 g (1 oz) butter
100 g (3½ oz) diced white bread

Rinse the cherries and remove the stems and stones. In a bowl, purée the cherries with three-quarters of the wine and half the sugar, using a hand mixer. In a saucepan, melt the butter and add the cherry purée, diced bread and the remainder of the wine and sugar. Let it simmer over a moderate heat until the mixture has thickened significantly. Pour into a serving bowl and refrigerate. When the pudding is chilled, decorate with edible flowers and white sugar crystals.

This recipe is from the *Forme of Cury* (c. 1390), created by the head chefs of Richard II of England, and a version has also been developed by Moira Buxton in *Medieval Cooking Today*.

Layered Almond Milk Pudding

200–250 g (7–9 oz) ground almonds
500 ml (1 pint) milk
4–5 gelatine leaves
100 g (3½ oz) sugar
50 ml cream, whipped
3 tbsp blueberries (use dark-blue berries)

In a saucepan, combine the milk, ground almonds and sugar. Bring to a boil, stirring, and leave to simmer over a moderate heat for 10 minutes. Soften the gelatine leaves in cold water, squeeze out any excess water and soak it in four tablespoons of the almond milk. Add the gelatine mixture to the saucepan, stirring. Remove from the heat. When the mixture has cooled, add the cream.

Extract the juice from the blueberries by crushing them through a sieve. Divide the pudding mixture into two portions and colour one of them with the blueberry juice. Pour the two puddings into a mould, one on top of the other, and refrigerate overnight. Carefully turn the mould over, and you will have a handsome, two-tone dessert. Decorate before serving, for example with red berries and mint leaves. If you wish to create an even more spectacular pudding, layer each colour twice. This recipe is based on the fourteenth-century cooking instructions by Taillevent in *Le Viandier*, with reference to *Das Kuchbuch der Sabrina Welserin*, from sixteenth-century Germany.

Another way to make a layered pudding:

> 1 litre (2 pints) almond milk (follow recipe on p. 186,
> but leave out the salt and use plenty of sugar instead)
> 10 12 gelatine leaves
> juice from 6 tbsp blueberries crushed through a sieve

Divide the almond milk in two and colour one portion with the blueberry juice. Add the gelatine leaves to each portion (2 x 5–6 leaves). Pour the mixtures into a mould, one colour on top of the other.

Apple Stew with Figs and Raisins

> 3–4 medium-sized apples
> 8–10 dried figs
> 140 g (1 cup) raisins
> 75 g (⅔ cup) coarsely ground nuts
> 200 ml (1 cup) water
> 150 ml (¾ cup) white wine
> 3–5 tbsp sugar
> 1 tsp ground ginger
> 1 tsp ground cinnamon
> ¼ tsp ground cloves
> ½ tsp ground black pepper
> pinch of ground saffron

Peel and cube the apples, and cut the figs into small pieces. In a saucepan, boil the apples, figs and raisins in the water and wine solution for approximately 15 minutes or until soft. Add the nuts, sugar and spices. Taste and adjust the seasoning, if needed. You could refrigerate the stew and serve it in a handsome dessert bowl together with almond cream (recipe below).

This recipe is based on the cooking instructions from the *Ménagier de Paris* collection for an accompaniment to fish dishes during days of fasting. It has also been developed by D. Eleanor Scully and Terence Scully in *Early French Cookery*.

Almond Cream

125 g (4½ oz) ground almonds
100 ml (½ cup) water
100 ml (½ cup) sweet white wine
300 ml (1½ cups) cream
2–3 tbsp sugar
⅓ tsp salt

Boil the ground almonds in the water for a moment, stirring. Then add the wine, salt, sugar and cream, and cook the mixture over a moderate heat, still stirring, until it has thickened and become creamy. Finally sieve the mixture, taste and add more sugar if necessary. Almond cream is served chilled; in the refrigerator, it will thicken further. You can serve almond cream with different pies or with fresh fruits and berries. This recipe has as a source Jukka Blomqvist and Auri Hakomaa's *Keskiajan keittiön salaisuudet*.

In medieval England almond milk or almond cream was usually offered at the beginning of the third course, followed by fritters. At the London wedding banquet for Henry IV of England and Joan of Navarre in 1403, for instance, the sweet delicacies served at the end of the meal were almond cream, pears in sugar syrup, fritters, cream puddings and pastries.

108 Two women collecting roses in the *Tacuinum sanitatis*. In the Middle Ages flowers were used as decorations, colourants and food flavouring in the same way as herbs. The shade of the food was determined by the colour of the inflorescence, provided that the colour was successfully transferred in the cooking process. While the ability of roses to give colour was non-existent, the flavoursome flowers worked well as ingredients in sweet puddings. Rose water was used as a sauce, and to flavour sweet bakery goods. Elderflowers, too, could be added to various pastries and elegant soups, and the cookery books mention primrose and hawthorn flowers as well. Blue or bluish-purple violets gave dishes a heavenly hue. The flowers could also be used to decorate various meat dishes such as spicy meatballs. Alternatively crushing boiled and dried violet petals in a mortar before thickening them in almond milk produced a completely separate dish. A striking contrast could be achieved by decorating saffron-tinted, golden-yellow jelly with violets. Naturally considerable symbolic significance was also invested in these flowers, which only added to their popularity, particularly on festive occasions. A blue violet stood for religious devotion, a purple violet for the sufferings of Christ, and a purplish-red violet for the heavenly kingdom. A three-coloured flower epitomized the Holy Trinity. In Christian allegory a red rose signified the blood of Christ, alongside heavenly love. It was also a symbol of the Virgin Mary. In secular symbolism the rose was a popular token of love – and still is to this day.

Rose Pudding

1 white rose
5–6 tbsp rice flour
250–300 ml (1–1¼ cups) milk
50 g (1¾ oz) sugar
¾ tsp ground cinnamon
¾ tsp ground ginger
550–600 ml (2¼–2½ cups) cream
pinch of salt
10 pitted, dried dates, chopped
1 tbsp pine nuts

Remove the petals from the corolla of the rose and discard the sepals. Soak the petals in hot water for a couple of minutes, then dry them carefully between two pieces of kitchen paper and place a flat weight on top. In a saucepan, combine the rice flour and a small amount of milk, stir into a smooth paste and add the remainder of the milk. Heat while stirring until the mixture has thickened. Remove from the hob and add the sugar, salt, spices and cream. Replace onto the burner and stir over a moderate heat until the mixture has thickened once more, but do not boil. Add the dates, pine nuts and rose petals, and stir for an additional couple of minutes. Pour into a serving bowl and let cool. Stir intermittently during the cooling process to avoid a skin forming on the surface. Refrigerate. Before serving, decorate with chopped dates, pine nuts and rose petals, or with an entire rose.

The original recipe stems from late fourteenth-century England, from the *Forme of Cury*, and a version has also been developed by Moira Buxton in *Medieval Cooking Today*.

Do not buy a greenhouse rose from a florist for the pudding, as cut roses raised for retail may contain harmful chemicals. I suggest you make the pudding in the summertime, when you can pick a rose for free in your own garden or in the wild. (However, avoid rose bushes close to busy main roads.) If the petals are sparse, use two roses instead of one.

Walnut and Date Pie

base:
450 ml (2 cups) medium-coarse wheat flour
½ tsp salt
125 g (4½ oz) butter
5 tbsp water

filling:
2 tbsp sugar
⅓ tsp ground cloves
1½ tbsp raisins
100 ml (½ cup) walnuts
100 ml (½ cup) pitted, dried dates, chopped
approx. 500 ml (1 pint) almond milk

Make a double portion of almond milk (recipe on p. 186), preferably rather thick. Prepare the pie base: with your fingertips, work the flour, salt and butter into a crumbly paste, to which you add the cold water, incorporating it quickly. Divide the dough into three parts, and one of those parts further into two, at which point you have four pieces of dough altogether. Press one of the large pieces onto the bottom and sides of a cake pan with a removable bottom (20–22 cm or 8–9 inches in diameter). Sprinkle with sugar and a pinch of cloves, and arrange the nuts evenly on top. Pour a small amount of almond milk onto this. Roll one of the smaller pieces of dough into a matching circle and place it over the bottom layer. Sprinkle with sugar and cloves, add the dates and pour a small amount of almond milk on top. Roll the second small piece of dough into a layer, and sprinkle with sugar. Arrange the raisins onto this layer and, again, pour some almond milk on top. Roll the second large piece of dough into a top layer and cover the pie. Bake on the lower rack of a 180°C (355°F) oven for approximately one hour.

This recipe is from fourteenth-century Italy, from *Libro della cucina del secolo XIV*, ed. Franceso Zambrini, and was developed by Odile Redon, Françoise Sabban and Silvano Serventi in *The Medieval Kitchen*. Almond cream (recipe on p. 202) is a fine accompaniment to this rich and moist pie, which can be served either chilled or at room temperature.

109 Tavern scene with men drinking wine – below, a cellarer is at work. According to medieval understanding, a virtuous and morally correct human being could be identified by the fact that he drank wine with caution during a formal meal, without succumbing to excessiveness on other occasions.

Currant and Almond Biscuits

200 g (7 oz) butter
9 tbsp brown sugar
1 egg
260 g (2 cups) flour
½ tsp grated lemon rind
½ tsp ground cardamom
9 tbsp ground almonds
1 cup currants

Preheat the oven to 180°C (355°F). Cream the butter and sugar until fluffy; stir in the egg. Combine the lemon rind, cardamom, sugar, almonds and currants with the flour, and add to the creamed butter. Mould into round, flat biscuits. If the dough sticks to your fingers, place it in the refrigerator for a while. Bake the biscuits on the middle rack of the oven for 10–12 minutes or until they have taken some colour. Let cool. This batch will yield two baking sheets of approximately 24 medium-sized biscuits.

This recipe has been developed in reference to Madeleine Pelner Cosman and The Oulu Medieval Association.

Pine Nut Fondants

200 g (7 oz) sugar
2 tbsp clear, runny honey
125 ml (¼ pint) water
1–1½ tbsp crushed pine nuts
around 100 g (3½ oz) soft white bread, crumbled
½–1 tsp ground ginger

In a saucepan, boil the sugar, honey and water over a moderate heat until syrupy. Remove from the heat and stir vigorously for a couple of minutes. Add the remainder of the ingredients. Moisten a shallow baking tray with water and pour the mixture into the dish. Leave to harden. Cut the fondant into pieces and serve. This recipe is based on the cooking instructions in the *Forme of Cury* and a version has also been developed by Moira Buxton in *Medieval Cooking Today*.

Drinks

Hippocras

1 litre (2 pints) red wine
150 g (5 oz) sugar
2 tsp ground cinnamon
2 tsp ground ginger
(optional: small piece of galangal, see p. 93)

Place a small amount of the wine in a saucepan together with the sugar, and heat until the sugar has melted, but do not boil it. In a separate bowl, combine the remainder of the ingredients; add the sweetened wine and leave

110 A housekeeper instructs her assistant in the art of preserving wine. The French poet Eustache Deschamps (1346–1406) listed 25 different types of wine that every able housewife was well advised to store in her wine cellar.

to stand for a couple of hours, stirring occasionally. Strain the wine several times through a folded piece of cheesecloth until the drink runs clear. Bottle, and consume after a day or two. You can also experiment with a pinch of ground nutmeg, pepper or even cloves for added flavour. This recipe is based on the instructions from the *Ménagier de Paris*. Odile Redon, Françoise Sabban and Silvano Serventi also provide a version in *The Medieval Kitchen*.

Claret

1 bottle white wine
100–200 ml (½–1 cup) honey
1 tbsp ground cinnamon
1 tbsp ground ginger
1 tbsp ground cardamom
1 tsp white pepper

In a saucepan, combine the wine and honey and heat to boiling point. Skim off any surface scum, check the sweetness and add the spices. Transfer the liquid to a bowl, cover with a lid and leave to brew for 24 hours. Strain the liquid through a piece of cheesecloth a couple of times. Bottle. The drink will be ready for consumption in one month's time, but is at its best after a year. This recipe is taken from the fourteenth century English *Forme of Cury* collection and has used as a source *Curye on Inglish* by Constance B. Hieatt and Sharon Butler.

Numerous spiced wines were known in the Middle Ages, of which *claret* or *clarrey* (from the French *claré* or *claree*) was the most commonly served after hippocras. The name originated from the Latin *vinum claratum*, meaning 'wine made clear'. Nowadays the designation refers to a dry red wine. More sophisticated versions (such as the Lord's Claret) included additional spices and a splash of *aqua vitae*. In medieval households spiced wines were usually brewed at home. The simplest method was to tie the spices in a cloth bag and put them to soak in a dish of wine.

111 In Dirk Bouts's fifteenth-century painting Melchizedek offers Abraham bread and wine as a token of his hospitality.

Sage Wine

2 tsp dried sage
1 litre (2 pints) dry white wine
100 ml (½ cup) clear distilled liquor
30 sugar cubes
2 cloves
2 bay leaves

Place the ingredients in an appropriate vessel, for instance a lidded household bucket. Leave the liquid to brew for one month, stirring occasionally. Strain the liquid and pour it into a clean glass bottle. This portion is fairly small, so you can double or treble it. Serve the drink chilled. Sage wine (*saugé* in French) is an excellent welcome drink. The original recipe dates from late fourteenth-century France, from the *Ménagier de Paris*.

Orange Wine

1 litre (2 pints) dry white wine
100–200 ml (½–1 cup) clear distilled liquor, such as vodka
peel from 3 oranges
200 g (7 oz) honey
1–2 tsp ground ginger

Wash and peel the oranges, and cut the peel into pieces. Leave the peel to soak in the gingered wine for two weeks. Add the honey and distilled liquor, strain and bottle the brew. Orange wine (*orangeat* in French) requires ageing, so drink it only after several months. It is a fine dessert drink.

Oranges were not sweet in the Middle Ages, but quite sour, almost comparable to lemons. Unpeeled oranges kept fairly well and were exported from the Mediterranean regions to other parts of Europe, both as whole fruits and fruit juices. The oranges and lemons imported into the Nordic countries were luxuries reserved for well-to-do households.

I have developed this recipe with reference to Josy Marty-Dufaut's *La Gastronomie du Moyen Age*.

Gingered Mead

1 litre (2 pints) water
1 kg (2 lb) honey
¹⁄₁₀ bag wine yeast
50 ml (1½ fl. oz) pale ale
piece of fresh ginger root (to taste)

Slice the ginger. In a saucepan, combine the water, honey and ginger slices, and boil for a while, skimming off any surface scum. Let cool to room temperature. Mix the yeast with the small amount of beer and add

112 Gnomes carry an enormous cluster of grapes in a miniature by Simon Bening.

to the saucepan. Leave to brew in a suitable container stored at room temperature for five weeks, stirring occasionally during the first two weeks.

Strain the liquid, taking care not to include any yeast remaining at the bottom of the container. Leave to brew for an additional three weeks. Bottle, again taking care not to include any remaining yeast sediment. Leave to brew for one more week, this time in a cool place. Serve chilled.

Minted mead (recipe below) is a faster alternative. I have used Sandra Årstrand's *Medeltida mat på modern svenska* as a source.

Minted Mead

4 litres (8½ pints) boiling water
250 g (9 oz) honey
250 g (9 oz) brown sugar
1–1½ lemons
½ tbsp fresh mint
5 g (1½ tsp) yeast
sugar
raisins

Wash the lemons thoroughly and peel a few thin strips of rind into a large, deep dish. Then peel the lemons completely, removing the pith. Slice and add to the dish together with the mint and brown sugar. Pour the boiling water on top. When the liquid has cooled to almost room temperature, add the honey and let it melt. Crumble in the yeast. Leave the solution to brew at room temperature for 24 hours.

Prepare a sufficient number of clean bottles and drop ½ tsp sugar and a few raisins into each. Add the liquid. Store the bottles in a cool place to brew into mead. The drink will be ready in four days.

During the course of the Middle Ages, mead lost its popularity in the more southerly parts of Europe, particularly among the aristocracy. The reason is believed to be the fact that mead was sooner seen as a medicinal drink. In many medieval recipe collections mead was indeed grouped with drinks suitable for the ailing. Juniper berry mead was the common man's wine in the Nordic countries.

Sources include The Finnish Association for Beekeepers (Suomen Mehiläishoitajain Liitto) and Anna-Liisa Neuvonen.

Caudell

1–2 egg yolks
300 ml (10 fl. oz) ale
3–5 tsp sugar
¼ tsp salt
pinch of ground saffron

In a saucepan, combine the egg yolks and ale. Heat, stirring constantly, until the mixture has thickened to the consistency of a milkshake. Do not allow it to boil. Add sugar to taste, a tiny amount of salt and a pinch of saffron. Serve warm without delay.

The recipe for this warm, ale-based drink originates in fifteenth-century England (Harleian MS 4016) and has been developed with reference to James L. Matterer's *Gode Cookery*:

Caudell. Take faire tryed yolkes of eyren, and cast in a potte; and take good ale,
or elles good wyn, a quantite, and sette it ouer þe fire
And whan hit is at boyling, take it fro þe fire, and caste pere-to saffron, salt,
Sugur; and ceson hit vppe, and serue hit forth hote.

List of Illustrations

1 Aristocratic couple, from a French edition of Giovanni Boccaccio, *The Decameron*, 15th century, Bibliothèque Nationale, Paris, MS 5070, f. 25.
2 Recipe for 'Blank Mang', British Library, London, Add. MS 5016, 1037.g.28.
3 Preparation for a feast; Prodigal Son Window, Scene 7, north transept, Chartres Cathedral, *c.* 1214.
4 The Limbourg Brothers, 'July', from *Très Riches Heures du Duc de Berry*, 1416, Musée Condé, Chantilly.
5 Farmhouse kitchen, *Taquinum sanitatis*, 1474, Bibliothèque Nationale, Paris, MS lat. 9333, fol. 97v.
6 'January', *Très Riches Heures du Duc de Berry*, 1416, Musée Condé, Chantilly
7 *Grandes chroniques de France de Charles V*, Bibliothèque Nationale, Paris, MS fr. 2813, fol. 473v.
8 Dirk Bouts, *The Last Supper*, 1464–8, St-Pierre, Louvain.
9 The peacock, showpiece of a royal or aristocratic meal; a reproduction of a medieval engraving in Paul Lacroix, *Mœurs, usages et costumes* (Paris, 1873).
10 Two kitchen helpers roast meat on a spit, from the *Luttrell Psalter*, 14th century, British Library, London, Add. MS 42130, fol. 206v.
11 Picking olives, *Tacuinum sanitatis*, 1474, Bibliothèque Nationale, Paris, MS lat. 9333, fol. 13v.
12 Selling offal at the market stall, *Tacuinum sanitatis*, 1474, Bibliothèque Nationale, Paris, MS lat. 9333, fol. 75.
13 Two fish, in a painting by Hieronymus Bosch (*c.* 1450–1516), Museum van der Bergh, Antwerp.
14 Fra Angelico, *The Angels Serve Food to St Dominic and the Monks*, predella of *The Coronation of the Virgin*, *c.* 1430, Louvre, Paris.
15 Gluttons in hell, woodcut from *Kalender of Shepherdes*, reproduction in facsimile edition of Guy Marchant [1493] (Paris, 1926).
16 Sobriety and Gluttony; British Library, London, Add. MS 28162, fol. 10v.
17 Diabolic temptations, *Le Breviari d'amor*, early 14th century.
18 Sign of Venus, *Kalender of Shepherdes*, reproduction in facsimile edition of Guy Marchant [1493] (Paris, 1926).
19 Bed-bound patient, British Library, London, MS. Royal 15 D I, fol. I.
20 A choleric, a sanguine, a melancholy and a phlegmatic; *Kalender of Shepherdes*, reproduction in facsimile edition of Guy Marchant [1493] (Paris, 1926).

21 *Queen Esther and King Ahasuerus*, tapestry originating probably from Tournai, 1460–70, Minneapolis Institute of Arts.

22 'August', from a Flemish calendar from the early 16th century, British Library, London, Add. MS 24098, fol. 25B.

23 Collecting rye, in Abu Khasim's *Observations sur la nature et les propriétés des aliments* (1390), Bibliothèque Nationale, Paris, MS n.a.l. 1673, fol. 47.

24 Two women preparing pasta, in Abu Khasim's *Observations sur la nature et les propriétés des aliments* (1390), Bibliothèque Nationale, Paris, MS n.a.l. 1673, fol. 50.

25 'November', from a Flemish calendar from the early 16th century, British Library, London, Add. MS 24098, fol. 28B.

26 Master of the Housebook, *The Last Supper*, c. 1480, Gemäldegalerie, Berlin.

27 A communal oven from the *Tacuinum sanitatis*, 1474, Bibliothèque Nationale, Paris, MS lat. 9333, fol. 61v.

28 'December', from a Flemish calendar from the early 16th century, British Library, London, Add. MS 24098, fol 29b.

29 A nobleman's garden in a Flemish illustration for the *Roman de la rose, c.* 1485, British Library, London, Harley MS 4425, f. 12v.

30 Preparing green vegetables, from the *Luttrell Psalter*, 14th century, British Library, London, Add. MS 42130, fol. 207.

31 Eden, in the 15th-century illumination of a work by Flavius Josephus, Bibliothèque Nationale, Paris, MS fr. 11, fol. 3v.

32 Collecting cabbage, *Tacuinum sanitatis*, 1474, Bibliothèque Nationale, Paris, MS lat. 9333, fol. 20.

33 Picking beans, *Tacuinum sanitatis*, 1390s, Österreichische Nationalbibliothek, Vienna, Codex Vindobonensis S. N. 2644, fol. 49.

34 Gold and silver vessels in an illustration from *De secretis secretorum*, 1326–7.

35 Pietro de' Crescenzi, *Le Rustican*, 1470, Bibliothèque Nationale, Paris (Arsenal), MS 5064, fol. 209v.

36 An ox, from the *Luttrell Psalter*, 14th century, British Library, London, Add. MS 42130, fol. 159v.

37 Birds are taken for plucking and cooking, in Paul Lacroix, *Mœurs, usages et costumes* (Paris, 1873).

38 Hieronymus Bosch, 'Gluttony', *The Seven Deadly Sins and Four Last Things*, 1475–80, Prado, Madrid.

39 Birds in a miniature by Évrard d'Espinques, from Bartholomeus Anglicus' *De proprietatibus rerum*, 1480, Bibliothèque Nationale, Paris, MS fr. 9140, fol. 211.

40 'November', from the *Heures de Charles d'Angoulême*, 1482–5, Bibliothèque Nationale, Paris, MS lat. 1173, fol. 6.

41 Seals of the Butchers' Guild at Bruges, 1356, Paul Lacroix, *Mœurs, usages et costumes* (Paris, 1873).

42 Cooked meat is carved and arranged onto serving platters, *Luttrell Psalter*, 14th century, British Library, London, Add. MS 42130, fol. 207v.

43 Gerard Horenbout, 'The Lord's Banquet', from the *Grimani Breviary*, 1510–20, Biblioteca Nazionale Marciana, Venice.

44 Sea creatures, *Ashmole Bestiary*, 13th century, Bodleian Library, Oxford, fol. 85.

45 Rimini Master, *The Banquet of St Guido with Bishop Geberardo of Ravenna*, 14th century,

Museum, Vienna.

72 Hieronymus Bosch, detail from *The Garden of Earthly Delights*, 1503–4, Prado, Madrid.

73 Fig seller by Évrard d'Espinques, from Bartholomeo Anglicus, *De proprietatibus rerum*, 15th century, Bibliothèque Nationale, Paris, MS fr. 9140, fol. 361v.

74 Nutcracker, from Paul Lacroix, *Moeurs, usages et costumes* (Paris, 1873).

75 Hieronymus Bosch, *The Marriage Feast at Cana*, Museum Boijmans Van Beuningen, Rotterdam.

76 'September', from the *Grimani Breviary*, 1510–20, Biblioteca Nazionale, Venice, MS lat. XI67 (7531), fol. 9v.

77 Wine drinking in the North, an engraving from Olaus Magnus, *Historia de gentibus septentrionalibus* (1555).

78 Inspecting and tasting a new vintage, from a Flemish calendar, early 16th century, British Library, London, Add. MS 24098, fol. 27v.

79 Brewer at work, from Paul Lacroix, *Moeurs, usages et costumes* (Paris, 1873).

80 Nordic decorative drinking vessels (*kousa*), Olaus Magnus, *Historia de gentibus septentrionalibus* (1555).

81 A cupbearer in a 15th-century manuscript illumination, Bibliothèque Nationale, Paris, MS fr. 9140, fol. 114.

82 Devil's bacchanal in a tavern, miniature by Jean Rolin in Henry Suso's *L'Orloge de sapience*, Bibliothèque Royale, Brussels, MS IV.III, fol. 38v.

83 Richard II dining, from the *Chronique d'Angleterre*, British Library, London, no. 115, vol. III, Royal 14 E. IV, fol. 265v.

84 Measures and weights, Olaus Magnus, *Historia de gentibus septentrionalibus* (1555).

85 A cook lifts lamb meat from the large cauldron, 13th century, Samuel, Old Testament.

86 Servants assemble the roasted meats while Bishop Odo is feasting, from the *Bayeux Tapestry*, *c.* 1077, Musée de la Tapisserie, Bayeux.

87 The Wedding at Cana, in the *Très Belles Heures de Notre-Dame du Duc Jean de Berry*, Bibliothèque Nationale, Paris, MS new acquisition lat. 3093, fol. 67v.

88 Demons and diners, mural, 1510–22, St Lawrence, Lohja, Finland.

89 Two bakers in a bakehouse, Bodleian Library, Oxford, Canon. Lit. 99, fol. 16.

90 Gerard David, *The Virgin with the Porridge Spoon*, 1515, Musées Royaux des Beaux-Arts, Brussels.

91 Picking leeks, medieval woodcut from *A Treasury of Bookplates*, ed. Fridolf Johnson (London, 1977).

92 'January', from the *Kalender of Shepherdes*, reproduction in facsimile edition of Guy Marchant [1493] (Paris, 1926).

93 Master Herbalrist in *Platearius*, Bibliothèque Nationale, Paris, MS fr. 9136, fol. iv.

94 'February', *Très Riches Heures du Duc de Berry*, 1416, Musée Condé, Chantilly.

95 Cockerels, partridges, and other birds in a miniature, 1290, *Heures à l'usage de Cambrai*, Bibliothèque Nationale, Paris (Arsenal), MS 1185, fol. 208.

96 Hare hunting as pictured in the hunting book of Gaston Phoebus, Bibliothèque Nationale, Paris, MS fr. 616, fol. 92.

97 The unmaking of a red deer, Gaston Phoebus, Bibliothèque Nationale, Paris, MS fr. 616, fol. 70.

This book also features a selection of non-captioned illustrations drawn exclusively from Olaus Magnus, *Historia de gentibus septentrionalibus* (1555) and Paul Lacroix, *Treasury of Medieval Illustrations* (Mineola, NY, 2008): *page* 12 A baron's banquet (from Lacroix); page 28 A Nordic market place (from Magnus); *page* 49 Harvesting in the North (from Magnus); *page* 61 Drinking cup decorated with precious stones (from Lacroix); *page* 70 Two-branched candlestick (from Lacroix); *page* 75 Hunting in Lappland (from Magnus); *page* 97 Physician from a *Danse Macabre*, 1490 (from Lacroix); *page* 135 Punishment of a drunkard (from Magnus).

Bibliography

Almond, Richard, *Medieval Hunting* (Phoenix Mill, 2003)

Austin, Thomas, *Two Fifteenth-Century Cookery-Books. Harleian* MS 279 & *Harl.* MS 4016, *with extracts from Ashmole* MS 1429, *Laud* MS 553, *and Douce* MS 55 (London, 1888)

Årstrand, Sandra, *Medeltida mat på modern svenska* (Värnamo, 2002)

Birlouez, Eric, *À la table des seigneurs, des moines et des paysans du Moyen Âge* (Rennes, 2011)

Bitch, Irmgard, Trude Ehlert and Xenja von Ertzdorff, *Essen und Trinken in Mittelalter und Neuzeit* (Simaringen, 1987)

Black, Maggie, *The Medieval Cookbook* (London, 1992)

Blomqvist, Jukka, and Auri Hakomaa, *Keskiajan keittiön salaisuudet. Tuokiokuvia, reseptejä, mausteita* (Helsinki, 2006)

Brereton, Georgine E., and Janet M. Ferrier, eds, *Le ménagier de Paris* (Oxford, 1981)

Buxton, Moira, *Medieval Cooking Today* (Buckinghamshire, 1983)

Bynum, Caroline Walker, *Holy Feast and Holy Fast. The Religious Significance of Food to Medieval Women* (Berkeley, CA, 1987)

Campbell, Å., *Det svenska brödet. En jämförande etnologisk-historisk undersökning* (Stockholm, 1950)

Camporesi, Piero, 'Bread of Dreams: Food and Madness in Medieval Italy', *History Today*, 39 (1989), pp. 14–21.

—, *The Magic Harvest: Food, Folklore and Society*, trans. Joan Krakover Hall (Cambridge, 1998)

Cummins, John, *The Hound and the Hawk : The Art of Medieval Hunting* (London, 1998)

Dawson, Thomas, *The Good Huswifes Jewell*, ed. Susan J. Evans (Albany, NY, 1988)

Ehlert, Trude, *Das Kochbuch des Mittelalters* (Zürich, 1990)

Ein Buch von Guter Spise, at http://cs-people.bu.edu/akatlas/Buch/buch.html

Fenton, Alexander and Eszter Kisban, eds, *Food Habits in Change. Eating Habits from the Middle Ages to the Present Day* (Edinburgh, 1986)

Fletcher, Nichola, *Charlemagne's Tablecloth: A Piquant History of Feasting* (New York, 2005)

Frati, Ludovico, ed., *Libro di cucina del secolo* XIV (Bologna, 1970)

Friedman, David and Elizabeth Cook, *Cariadoc's Miscellany*, at www.pbm.com/~lindahl/cariadoc/recipe_toc.html

Grönholm, Kirsti, 'Simaa ja suolakalaa', *Hopeatarjotin*, 1 (1995)

Hajek, Hans, *Daz Buoch von guoter Spize* (Berlin, 1958)

Häkkinen, Kaisa, and Terttu Lempiäinen, *Agricolan yrtit* (Turku, 2007)

Hartola, Marja, 'Kasknauriit, sualsilakka ja kyrsä arken – sallatti, setsuuri ja lantloora pirois, varsinaissuomalaista ruokataloutta 1000 vuoden ajalta', *Pöytä on katettu*, 27 (2004), pp. 7–30

—, *Ruokaretki Turun saaristoon* (Jyväskylä, 2004)

Heers, Jacques, *Fêtes des fous et carnavals* (Paris, 1997)

Helenius, Johanna, 'Turun linnan ruokatalous Juhana Herttuan aikana', *Turun maakuntamuseon raportti 16. Tutkimuksia Turun linnasta*, 1 (Vammala, 1994)

Henisch, Bridget Ann, *The Medieval Cook* (Woodbrige, 2009)

Hieatt, Constance B., 'The Middle English Culinary Recipes in MS Harley 5401: An Edition and Commentary', *Medium Ævum*, LXV/1 (1996), pp. 54–71

—, ed., *An Ordinance of Pottage. An Edition of the Fifteenth Century Culinary Recipes in Yale University's MS Beinecke 163* (London, 1988)

Hieatt, Constance B., and Sharon Butler, *Curye on Inglish: English Culinary Manuscripts of the Fourteenth Century* (New York, 1985)

Hieatt, Constance B., Brenda Hosington and Sharon Butler, *Pleyn Delit: Medieval Cookery for Modern Cooks* (Toronto, 1996)

Impelluso, Lucia, *La natura e i suoi simboli. Piante, fiori e animali* (Milan, 2005)

Jansen-Sieben, Ria, and Johanna Maria van Winter, eds, *De keuken van de late midde-leeuwen* (Amsterdam, 1998)

Kjersgaard, Erik, *Mad og øl i Danmarks middelalder* (Odense, 1978)

Klemettilä, Hannele, *Keskiajan keittiö* (Jyväskylä, 2007)

—, *Mansimarjasta punapuolaan. Marjakasvien kulttuurihistoriaa* (Helsinki, 2011)

Krötzl, Christian, 'Paavin keittiö. Keskiajan paavillisen kuurian arkea ja juhlapäivää', *Herkullista historiaa. Kulttuurisia makupaloja Italian keittiöistä kautta aikojen*, ed. Andreo Larsen, Liisa Savunen and Risto Valjus (Hämeenlinna, 2004), pp. 111–21

Das Kuchbuch der Sabina Welserin (1553), at www.daviddfriedman.com/Medieval/Medieval.html

Lagerqvist, L. O., and Nils Åberg, *Mat och dryck i forntid och medeltid* (Stockholm, 1994)

Landouzy, Louis, and Roger Pépin, eds, *Le régime du corps de maître Aldebrandin de Sienne: Texte français du XIIIe siècle* (Geneva, 1978)

Laurioux, Bruno, *Les livres de cuisine médiévaux* (Turnhout, 1997)

—, *Le Moyen Age à table* (Paris, 1989)

—, ed., 'Le "Registre de cuisine" de Jean de Bockenheim, cuisinier du pape Martin V', *Mélanges de l'École Française de Rome: Moyen Age, Temps Modernes*, C/2 (1988), pp. 709–60

—, *Le règne de Taillevent. Livres et pratiques culinaires à la fin du Moyen Âge* (Paris, 1997)

Le Goff, Jacques, *Medieval Civilization, 400–1500*, trans. Julia Barrow (Oxford, 1988)

Lehtonen, Ulla, *Luonnon hyötykasvien keruu- ja käyttöopas* (Porvoo, 1987)

Maestro Martino, 'Libro de arte coquinaria, Arte della cucina', in *Libri di ricette: Testi sopra lo scalco, il trinciante e i vini dal XIV al XIX secolo*, 2 vols, ed. Emilio Faccioli (Milan, 1966), pp. 117–204

Magnus, Olaus, *Historia de gentibus septentrionalibus* (Stockholm, 1909–25)

Mäkipelto, Anne, *Gastronominen ylellisyys myöhäiskeskiajan Italiassa ja Englannissa* (Licentiate's thesis, University of Jyväskylä, 1996)

Malaguzzi, Silvia. *Food and Feasting in Art*, trans. Brian Phillips (Los Angeles, CA, 2008)

Mänd, Anu, *Urban Carnival. Festive Culture in the Hanseatic Cities of the Easter Baltic, 1350–1550* (Turnhout, 2005)

Marchant, Guy, ed., *Le compost et Kalendrier des bergiers* [1493], facsimile edition (Paris, 1926)

Marty-Dufaut, Josy, *La Gastronomie du Moyen Age. 170 recettes adaptées à nos jours* (Marseille, 1999)

Matterer, James L., *Gode Cookery,* www.godecookery.com

Mead, William Edward, *The English Medieval Feast* (New York, 1967)

Menjot, Denis, ed., *Manger et boire au Moyen Age* (Paris, 1984)

Mennel, Stephen, *All Manner of Food: Eating and Taste in England and France from the Middle Ages to the Present* (Chicago, 1996)

Mestre Robert, *Libre del coch. Tractat de cuina medieval,* ed. Veronica Leimgruber (Barcelona, 1982)

Montanari, Massimo, *The Culture of Food,* trans. Carl Ipsen (Oxford, 1996)

Mulon, Marianne, ed., 'Liber de coquina. Deux traités inédits d'art culinaire médiéval', *Bulletin Philologique et Historique,* vol. 1 (Paris, 1971), pp. 396 420

Oulun keskiaikaseura, *Keskiaikaisia reseptejä,* at http://tols17.oulu.fi/~pkeisane/sivut/kokkaus.html

Pastoureau, Michel, *Une histoire symbolique du Moyen Âge occidental* (Paris, 2004)

Platina, Battista (Bartolomeo), *De Honesta Voluptate et Valetudine,* ed. and trans. Mary Ella Milham (Tempe, AZ, 1998)

Pleij, Herman, *Dreaming of Cockaigne: Medieval Fantasies of the Perfect Life,* trans. Diane Webb (New York, 2001)

Redon, Odile, Françoise Sabban and Silvano Serventi, *The Medieval Kitchen: Recipes from France and Italy,* trans. Edward Schneider (Chicago, IL, 1998)

Renfrow, Cindy, *Take a Thousand Eggs or More: A Collection of 15th century Recipes,* vols I–II (n. p., 1997)

Salisbury, Joyce E., *The Beast Within: Animals in the Middle Ages* (New York, 1994)

Santanach, Joan, *The Book of Sent Soví: Medieval Recipes from Catalonia,* trans. Robin Vogelzang (Barcelona, 2008)

Savelli, Mary, *Taste of Anglo-Saxon England* (Norfolk, 2002)

Scully, D. Eleanor, and Terence Scully, *Early French Cookery: Sources, History, Original Recipes and Modern Adaptations* (Ann Arbor, MI, 1998)

Scully, Terence, *The Art of Cookery in the Middle Ages* (Woodbridge, 1995)

—, ed., *Chiquart's 'On Cookery'. A Fifteenth-Century Savoyard Culinary Treatise* (New York, 1986)

—, 'Du fait de cuisine par Maistre Chiquart 1420', *Vallesia,* 40 (1985), pp. 101–231

—, *The Neapolitan Recipe Collection: Cuoco Napoletano* (Ann Arbor, MI, 2000)

—, *The Viandier of Taillevent: An Edition of all Extant Manuscripts* (Ottawa, 1988)

—, *The Vivendier: A Critical Edition with English Translation* (Totnes, 1997)

The Society of London Antiquaries, eds, *Ancient Cookery, A Collection of the Ordinances and Regulations for the Government of the Royal Household made in Divers Reigns from King Edward III to King William and Queen Mary also Receipts in Ancient Cookery* (London, 1740)

Spencer, Colin, *The Heretic's Feast: A History of Vegetarianism* (London, 1996)

Stouff, Louis, *Ravitaillement et alimentation en Provence aux XIVe et XVe siècles* (Paris, 1970)

Talve, Ilmar, *Kansanomaisen ruokatalouden alalta* (Helsinki, 1961)

Talvi, Jussi, *Gastronomian historia* (Helsinki, 1989)

Tannahill, Reay, *Food in History* (New York, 1973)

Tourunen, Auli, 'Animals in an Urban Context: A Zooarchaeological study of the Medieval and Post-medieval town of Turku', PhD thesis, University of Turku (2008)

Vilkuna, Anna-Maria, *Kruunun taloudenpito Hämeen linnassa 1500-luvun puolivälissä* (Helsinki, 1998)

Zambrini, Fancesco, ed., *Libro della cucina del secolo XIV* (Bologna, 1968)

Acknowledgements

The original Finnish text was first translated by Anne Stauss, and then modified and rearranged by the author. A sample translation was partially funded by FILI, the Finnish Literature Exchange.

Index